How to Save on Your Taxes Without Cheating

By

Adam Starchild

Books for Business
New York - Hong Kong

How to Save on Your Taxes Without Cheating

by Adam Starchild

ISBN 0-89499-029-2

Copyright © 2001 by Adam Starchild

Books for Business
New York - Hong Kong

http://www.businessbooksinternational.com

Contents

THE WEALTH ACCUMULATION TRUST: YOU DON'T HAVE TO LEAVE THE COUNTRY TO FIND A TAX HAVEN

THE COMPANY YOU KEEP

There's No Business Like Your Own Business.

The key to extraordinary financial achievement in the capitalist economic system often starts with the establishment of your own successful business. When you start a profitable enterprise it quickly promotes expanding "growth equity" -- literally, the measure of the increased value of your business -- and greater equity means access to the kind of financing you need to prosper even more. That's the miracle of business equity; it continues to multiply many times over, spurred by good management and wise reinvestment of profits.

There can be another profitable aspect to managing your own business that is not always readily apparent to the novice. Even if your efforts never produce a profit, engaging in a "business" can cut personal costs and tax liability considerably, often spelling the difference between financial independence, or continuation of a dreary life as someone else's wage slave.

A closely-held small business can be one of the best personal tax shelters available and, contrary to what you may have heard, starting your own enterprise doesn't necessarily require a radical drop in current income.

There are two well-established, proven methods by which a smart, ambitious individual can profit from personal business ownership while still retaining a current job; converting to independent contractor status and/or managing an additional "sideline" business. Often, both go hand in hand successfully. We'll have more to say about both possibilities in just a few moments.

Labor Trends Are With You

The historic, traditional employment pattern in America for many years saw millions of workers going to work, Monday through Friday, at an office, store or factory where, in theory, each employee put in his or her eight hours and perhaps some overtime, then went home.

That may have been the way it once was, but no more.

United States national population and labor trends have produced many new and attractive opportunities for part-time work, as well as for working in your own home. Single parents and families pinched for spending money in a time of declining buying power often must work two or three jobs just to make ends meet. The growth rate of the American labor force has declined by half during the decade of the 90's, a time when the post-World War II "baby boom" generation has matured and gone to work. Another major change; two-thirds of new entrants into the work force during this decade are women, many of them working mothers.

Such labor policy developments bode well for working parents who wish to balance work and family without sacrificing either. Industry can no longer afford to ignore issues such as child care, flex-time, and part-time work. Once considered narrowly as "women's issues," companies now realizing these are "people issues" and part of a trend to which they must respond or lose.

In responding and adapting to these radical new employment patterns smart companies are merely facing reality. Employers need workers and to be profitable, they simply have no choice but to bend with the times.

U.S. West, one of the "Baby Bell" regional telephone companies, openly competes for women workers, offering flexible work arrangements to lure skilled employees in a shrinking labor force. The company instituted one of the most liberal part-time work policies in the United States and all employees are eligible. The company even actively seeks outsiders for part-time work. Compensation and benefits are prorated on actual time worked, titles are preserved and promotions are possible. Managers, too, are allowed to work part-time. The IRS ruled in 1994 that in certain instances part time employees must be included within a company's pension and retirement plans, a point you should check with your employer if you are considering that work status.

These corporate policies make dollars and sense because they attract and retain talented employees who are able to devote more time to their families, without reducing commitment to their jobs. While all this may seem slightly astonishing conduct on the part of a large corporation, like many companies, U.S. West can't afford to do less. If they don't offer these opportunities -- "yes, we'll hire you on a part-time basis" and/or "yes, you can work at home" -- they stand to lose big in productivity and profits. Companies that fail to offer the new employment flexibility will undoubtedly lose out to more enlightened competition.

Flexible work arrangements are not without precedent in America. For many decades travelling sales people have prospered as semi- autonomous workers, setting their own schedules and hours, so long as they produce sales.

If people like you, professionals with specialized expertise, are in short supply in your particular geographic area, local companies undoubtedly will be eager to accommodate you, either as a part time employee or as an independent contractor. Skilled engineers, scientists and workers with technical "know-how" are difficult to find, so most companies strive to attract and retain these highly skilled individuals.

Many other corporations are now following the example set by U.S. West. About five hundred of Hewlett-Packard's 50,000 American employees now work part-time, half of them professionals and twenty-one are managers. Modern "high-tech" companies especially have much to gain by promoting work-at-home options for their workers and they are among the biggest boosters of this new labor concept. Working at home with personal computers and modems means increased sales of PCs, peripheral equipment and services, so high-tech companies stand to gain both financial and personnel benefits from this work trend.

Government is also getting into the act. The bureaucrats have finally realized "full-time" jobs actually can be accomplished on a part-time basis if individual workers are highly motivated and organized, qualities in short supply in most government offices. The federal civil service system now sanctions part-time work for federal employees, called "flex time" with formal procedures to allowing shifts from one government job to another to accommodate such requests. More than 7,000 New York state employees officially work part-time and the N.Y. Civil Service Department has a registry to match up available jobs with individuals wishing to work less than full schedules.

What You Need and What You'll Get

What all this means to you personally depends on whether you chose to develop your own business, or to switch to a part-time and/or home-work relationship with your present or a future employer. In either case, the opportunities for fundamental change in your work and life style are immense. With a little effort and knowledge, you could instantly become a part of the exciting trends that are fast changing in preparation for the 21st century American work experience.

Working part-time at your employer's place of business, or at home for one or several employers can be the useful first, transitional step towards becoming an independent contractor and running your own business.

Having your own business means potential freedom and financial independence. At the beginning, business success requires strong, unwavering motivation, realistic, no-

nonsense planning, a competitive spirit and the sustained personal energy to achieve well-thought out, specific goals.

That means prior planning is essential for survival and success. The market must be studied to determine if there is a demand for your skills, services or, if you're thinking of sales, to find out the true potential of your product. How about start-up costs and operating expenses? Take an honest look at your finances and be prepared to operate at a loss for a while after you start out on your own. How much money will you need originally and for how long before you show a profit? Are finances readily available, or should you borrow? How much income do you project and what will be the cash flow?

Many of these questions are answered in series of handy booklets with titles like "Business Plan for Small Business Firms," "Checklist for Going into Business," and "The Business Plan for Home-based Business," all published by the U.S. Small Business Administration and available from the Consumer Information Center, P.O. Box 100, Pueblo, Colorado 81002. Ask for the "Small Business Directory," which lists SBA publications and videos and their prices. You can also call the SBA Small Business Answer Desk at 1-800-U-ASK-SBA, (1-800-827-5722) for further information on available material.

In addition to book learning, there's the need for the right mental and psychological attitude. Make sure you're moving into an activity you really love. Don't just trade a dull job for something that doesn't really ignite your professional passions. Be ready for possible rejection and failure, and to modify, scrap and change your original ideas and plans. You must be ready, willing and able to put in vast amounts of time developing your ideas and then, once you begin, doing work, work and more work.

You may also have to retrain yourself in many areas, developing computer skills, mastering management of taxes and accounts, learning how to set and live by schedules.

"Sideline Business" or Hobby?

If you're hesitant about leaving the security of your present job, you can begin by experimenting with a sideline business in your spare time. Just create a new business out of activities you enjoy doing or are already doing on a part time basis. There are numerous "sideline business" possibilities; real estate, accounting, free-lance writing, graphic art, auto repair, teaching night school and student tutoring. For example, if you enjoy producing arts and craft objects for friends and relatives, expand and sell these products at flea markets and fairs. Locate distant craft shows, combine your new business with a vacation, then write off as business deduction not only craft supplies you would buy anyway, but part of your vacation expense as well.

In certain cases it is traditional for the IRS to attempt to eliminate business expense deductibility and other tax benefits based on a claim a given activity is not truly a business, but rather a "sideline" personal endeavor that only amounts to a hobby.

When the IRS declares a sideline business to be a hobby, it means total deductions are limited to whatever profit can be earned from that hobby, in other words, a "break even" situation. In effect, this means the sideline business income is tax-free, but the business owner is not allowed to create a loss by deducting non-cash expenses such as depreciation on equipment. And sideline business income cannot be distributed among family members so as to reduce the business owner's total taxable income.

As with everything else in tax law, there are ways to avoid having a sideline business treated by the IRS as a hobby. The Internal Revenue Code, in Section 530 of the 1978 Revenue Act, contains a "safe harbor" rule that says a sideline business that shows a profit in three out of any five consecutive years can be considered a legitimate business rather than a hobby. Certain special exceptions apply. For example, if you breed horses, the safe harbor rule requires three profitable years out of any seven consecutive years in order to qualify as a business for tax purposes.

Business taxpayers also can come within the safe harbor rule if they can prove they are trying to make a profit. Such proof is shown by documentation of paid advertising, promotion, sales proposals, market research, and the like. If you are a writer or in sales, save your rejection letters.

Based on tax court decisions, the most important factor in determining that a sideline business is eligible for business tax treatment is proof it is conducted in a professional manner. This means your business must be run like other similar enterprises ("an industry practice" as the IRS calls it) and it also means you must keep complete records to show this fact.

Ways to Do Business

When a person living in America chooses to go into business for him or herself, the law offers four major options so far as the choice of form in which the business will be conducted. Each form has merits and demerits and the new entrepreneur should weigh each carefully before making a choice.

These four choices include three forms that are time-tested and well established, the sole proprietorship, the partnership, the corporation and a newer form, the limited liability company.

There are about 20 million individual businesses in the United States and about 14 million operate as sole proprietorships. Nearly 2 million are partnerships. The rest are corporations. The mystery is why any good business person would avoid the corporate form, since sole proprietors and partners (and all their personal property) are totally exposed to any claims that can arise from doing business.

The Sole Proprietorship

You can choose any one of the four major methods of doing business, but one of the most common and least complicated is the single individual who simply offers his or her services to the public without any formal legal design. Such people are considered by the law to be **sole proprietors**, usually specialists in a craft or trade working by themselves, or with a few employees or independent contractors to assist them.

Any type of activity can be involved, but usually the operation is a small business enterprise -- perhaps a secretarial service conducted from a person's home, a free lance writer, a yard and landscape service, or a one or two person house painting and small contracting operation.

There are no formal requirements for a person to become a sole proprietorship, just start working and do what is necessary to keep the business going and hopefully make a profit. However the law forbids sole proprietors to represent themselves to the general public in a manner indicating they are either a corporation or partnership, each a legal status with defined rights upon which customers can rely.

Usually a sole proprietor uses a business or trade name, but documents and bank accounts will state that it is "John Smith, d.b.a. Smith Lawn Service." The "d.b.a." means "doing business as" and denotes the sole proprietorship. Most states have lists of existing trade names and in some states the use of a name can be reserved. Check with your state agency to see if there are any conflicts with your proposed name and existing trade names.

Beware! There is a major drawback in doing business as a sole proprietor; every bit of a sole proprietor's personal and business property is subject to attachment and seizure for business debts or other claims arising out of the business. This not only means an owner's personal assets are exposed, but business property can be attached by the owner's personal creditors. It is not unusual in this situation for personal and business accounts and property to be commingled, possibly endangering both when claims are made against them.

All net income from the business must be treated as personal income on the individual proprietor's tax return. While business expenses are deductible, state and federal taxes are imposed on the business income as part of the personal earnings of the owner, and must be declared as such, often at a higher tax rate.

The sole proprietorship may be a reasonable form to get started, but it is not recommended for any business owner seeking asset protection, or for those with increasing income and expanding sales or services.

While you don't need a lawyer to form a sole proprietorship -- you do it by your own actions -- you may need one to help you with the eventual problems resulting from a risky business operation of this nature.

The Partnership

One of the earlier definitions of a partnership describes it as "a contract between two or more competent persons to place their money, effects, labor and skill, and some or all of them, in lawful commerce or business, and to divide the profit and bear the loss in certain proportions."

Forming a general or limited partnership, particularly a "family partnership" -- one of the best known variations --

can reduce federal and state income and inheritance taxes, and, if it is done right, can provide maximum personal insulation from lawsuits and other potential liabilities.

Used successfully in the United States for almost two centuries, the continuing popularity of the limited partnership among knowledgeable financial planners attests to its effectiveness in protecting assets -- but only if properly organized and operated as the law requires.

In the broadest sense, a "**general partnership**," as it is called, is an association of two or more persons (or other legal entities) formed to conduct a business for mutual profit. In general partnerships, each partner is an equal co-owner, jointly running the business with the objective of a profit, each acting as agents for, and having a fiduciary relationship with one another, and as a result -- and here's the catch -- each partner is **personally liable** for the acts of the others, including partnership debts and liabilities.

In general partnerships, by common agreement, partners may have the same or differing capital investments, and may share profits and losses in the same or varying proportions, usually corresponding to each one's original investment. A partnership is recognized by the law for most purposes including making contracts, obtaining credit, filing bankruptcy, incurring debt, marshalling assets, and acquiring and transferring property, but a partnership, as such, does not pay tax -- its partners do as individuals owing income tax on their share of partnership income.

General partnerships (as compared to limited partnerships), also present some major problems: each general partner can be held personally liable for all partnership debts, or liabilities resulting from another partner's, or an agent's negligent or harmful acts. General partnerships often must be dissolved when one partner files personal bankruptcy or dies, unless immediate arrangements are made for a buy out of that partner's interest, or unless the partnership agreement anticipates such events and makes contingent continuation provisions. Usually a deceased general partner's interest is subjected to estate probate, often a lengthy and cumbersome process -- and estate and inheritance taxes are levied on the value of that interest, diminishing what goes to the heirs.

Then there's the **"limited partnership"** composed of at least one general partner (who is usually the managing partner), and one or more "limited partners," sometimes also called "special partners." The limited partner, who must take no part in the day-to-day management, has no personal liability beyond the amount of his or her agreed cash or other capital investment in the partnership. The limited partner does have a right to receive agreed amounts of partnership income when it is distributed. This arrangement is accomplished by specific written provisions in the partnership agreement, the basic document governing the partnership to which all partners are parties.

The legal relationship popularly known as a **"family partnership"** usually is created as a vehicle to transfer income and assets from the owner/organizer of a family business, or any one who accumulates valuable assets -- or is in a high income tax bracket -- to members of his or her own family so as to limit everyone's personal and tax liability to the maximum extent possible.

A "family partnership" is really nothing more than a limited partnership in which family members, rather than non-family business associates, are the limited partners, usually with a parent or grandparent as the managing general partner.

Unfortunately, this arrangement comes with the potential for all the usual intramural contact sports for which families are notorious, as well as the great advantages close relationships also make possible.

By comparison to establishing a family "corporation," which many use to protect assets, a family limited partnership offers the advantages of an agreement allowing the parties great precision in defining their rights, allows withdrawal of property with far fewer tax problems, and has no stockholders restrictions.

A family limited partnership has great potential as a shelter from creditors for both personal and family business assets, and certainly it can help to reduce estate and inheritance taxes. Income taxes can also be reduced substantially as family partnership income is spread among all partner/family members, including younger members with less income, meaning a lower overall family income tax rate.

But limited partnerships, family-based or otherwise, come at a very high price.

You must be exceedingly careful in complying with all local and state laws and regulations governing registration, firm names, and use of fictitious business names. Separate partnership bank accounts must be established with legal control of the funds clearly indicated. If a donee is to be a limited partner, his or her partnership interest must be reflected in all insurance policies, deeds, leases, business contracts and in any litigation which might occur. All statutory documentary requirements must be scrupulously met, and complete financial records maintained on an annual basis. Taxes return must be filed. Most importantly, when donee interests are involved, the donor must fully transfer to the donee all right, title and interest in order to avoid tax or legal contests of the partnership status.

Unless carefully crafted by experienced legal experts, your partnership may be vulnerable to IRS officials or creditors eager to use legal loopholes to destroy your protection. That could mean that after you are gone, and well after creating an ostensible "family partnership," your family may find itself in a financial and asset situation far worse than if nothing had been done. But this form of asset ownership and business has been around for two hundred years -- the problems (and the way around them) are well known and can be avoided. There are no "short cuts" but there are many possible rewards.

Limited Liability Companies

A new form of business entity, the "limited liability company" (LLC) that seeks to combine the best features of the corporation and the partnership has become available in most states and the District of Columbia. As of 1995, all states had adopted LLC statutes except Hawaii.

A **"limited liability company"** provides corporate limitation of liability against claims made on personal assets, but also gives the preferred pass-through tax status of a partnership to corporate share owners. Formation costs are usually similar to corporate formation costs.

In some ways a limited liability company acts much like a Subchapter S corporation, by passing through income, losses and attendant tax advantages to shareholders, but it is more flexible than the Subchapter S corporation because there are no restrictions on who may hold shares in a limited liability company.

The limited liability company can have a mixture of owners -- individuals, corporations, trusts, non-resident aliens, non-profit foundations. There are also fewer paper work and record keeping formalities with an LLC.

The major difficulties with LLCs is that this form of doing business is so relatively new, dating back only to Wyoming's 1977 statute, it will be years before its full advantages and disadvantages emerge from experience with its operation. There are many unresolved questions about legal powers and tax rule application that won't be decided about LLCs for many years as the courts address these issues.

Generally the LLC does seem to offer the potential as a flexible business or investment vehicle that can accommodate personal control requirements, achieve lower taxes and provided limited personal liability to the owners.

A professional incorporation service can also handle the formation a limited liability company for you, if you decide that is the best choice for your business operation.

INDEPENDENT CONTRACTORS

Under the 1935 National Labor Relations Act (NLRA), also known as the "Wagner Act" (named for the late New York Senator who was its chief congressional sponsor), for purposes of federal labor law, an **"employee"** is any person earning wages, salaries or commissions, not including farm workers, domestic servants, people working for their spouse or parent, railroad employees (covered by their own law) and **independent contractors**.

The Wagner Act was the first national law declaring the rights of workers to organize and join labor unions, bargain collectively and to have protection against certain employer actions defined as "unfair labor practices." As important as the NLRA is, its interpretation of an "employee" is not the most important definition when it comes to defining an independent contractor for tax purposes.

Far more important, the Internal Revenue Service expansively defines "employee" in section 3121(d)(2) of the

Internal Revenue Code as any individual who under, "the usual common law rules applicable" to employers and workers "has the status of employee." If that sounds highly open-ended, it is. There are no formal "common law rules," and the phrase itself refers to the mass of individual court and executive branch decisions handed down over many years in case rulings involving employees. As you will see, the IRS prefers that all workers be considered "employees" rather than independent contractors because it makes income tax collecting a lot easier for them.

In evaluating the facts of each case, the IRS uses a list of twenty factors or criteria to judge whether a given worker is an "employee" or an "independent contractor." A violation of any one of these highly subjective rules allows the IRS to reclassify a worker from the status of independent contractor to that of employee.

The essential test is whether management has the right to supervise and control the manner and means of work done by an individual. The employer need not actually exercise this power; it is enough that he or she has the right to do so. If so, the IRS says the worker is an "employee." If a worker clearly controls his or her own work methods, works for multiple employers, sets his own hours, is liable to suffer loses or make a profit and provides his or her own equipment, the

IRS will usually concede this person to be an independent contractor.

On the other hand, an "employee" usually must comply with the boss's instructions, renders personal service, works at his employer's place of business and uses tools or equipment the employer provides. He also can be fired or quit at any time.

Another difference: an injured "employee" is covered by statutory workman's compensation laws, but an "independent contractor" is not.

A true independent contractor controls his or her own hours worked and is paid when a product is finished, not by an hourly wage. The client cannot dictate how a contractor reaches a final result and his only legitimate concern is the quality and timeliness of the product. The independent needs more than just one client. Working 90 percent of the time for a former employer is sure to support an IRS finding of an employment relationship.

The independent must have home or other office removed from an employer's business premises and pay for his or her own office supplies and equipment. A written contract covering all these points is essential and may be accomplished by a simple "letter of agreement" outlining the product to be delivered, the due date, and the fee to be paid by the client.

The IRS assumes certain designated types of workers are independent contractors (professionals like doctors, lawyers, engineers, accountants, architects, consultants, real estate agents, direct sales persons, and some artisans like carpenters and plumbers), while most other workers are presumed to be employees.

The IRS automatically classifies certain other types of workers as employees under a "statutory" definition, including drivers who distribute goods and services such as meats, vegetables, bakery goods, beverages, laundry and dry cleaning; also full-time insurance sales people, home workers who perform work according to an employer's exact specifications, and full-time traveling sales people.

For example, today's "temporary workers," now a very important labor phenomenon, are independent contractors in relation to the work places where they are assigned to work, although they may be employees of their "temp" company, depending on the terms of their contract.

Unfortunately, in an amendment contained in Section 1706 of the Tax Reform Act of 1986, Congress said in effect that technical workers contracted for through a third party broker, such as engineers and computer programmers, cannot be treated as independent contractors. This section of the law has caused massive confusion and badly hurt technical consulting companies and smaller businesses who want part time assistance of this nature. Congressional legislation to correct this problem is now being considered.

An Important Distinction

The distinction between these two worker groups is important because the status of a worker defines his or her rights and remedies in various situations, including, most importantly for the IRS, whose obligation it is to pay unemployment, income withholding and Social Security taxes. An independent contractor is responsible for filing and paying his or her own taxes, whereas the employer must do this on behalf of an employee.

Because tax revenue is at stake, the IRS constantly checks business firms to see whether workers listed as independent contractors should really be treated as employees. The tax treatment of the two groups is quite different. The IRS prefers to collect taxes on employees from companies because employers are seen as more efficient and reliable taxpayers and easier to control, compared to independent contractors who are on their own and virtually unchecked (and uncheckable) by the IRS.

Rather than trying to reclassify millions of independent contractors one by one, the IRS takes the easier route of attacking the employment status of workers for the thousands of companies who employ independent contractors.

From 1988 to 1994, the IRS conducted 11,400 audits of firms forcing the reclassification of nearly 500,000 as employees rather than independent contractors, producing an additional $751 million in payroll taxes and penalties. Studies show that IRS rulings support "employee" status 90 percent of the time. The IRS is no respecter of size. Audits range from International Business Machines, Inc. (IBM), right down to the "mom and pop" enterprises.

Special targets have been truckers, florists, travel agents, computer programmers and even ministers of the faith.

Here's some 1995 cases reported in the media: Texas A&M College admitted it had paid 400 farm workers as independent contractors when they were in reality employees. The college was socked with $86,000 in back taxes. A New York City travel agency, Pisa Brothers Travel, had to pay $274,000 after agents were ruled to be workers. Paddock Publications, Inc. of Arlington Heights, Ill. is fighting a $5.6

million retroactive assessment based on reclassification of 1,500 newspaper employees including delivery men. That amount includes a $1 million fine. The company, operating on a small profit margin, says it will have to file bankruptcy if the IRS persists.

According to the **Wall Street Journal**, "Small companies are bearing the brunt of the IRS crackdown because they frequently fail to report free-lance employees, which encourages [these independent] contractors to conceal income." The IRS claims rather grandly that tax-evading independent contractors owed the government $30 billion for the 1993 tax year alone, but that estimate is disputed by outside experts.

Businesses suddenly found to have retroactive liability for "employees" treated as independent contractors face enormous dollar amounts for withholding, Social Security and other taxes, sometimes going back for many years. In IBM's case, as far back as 1986.

Taxes and the Independent Contractor

Whatever the tax problems faced by employers who hire "independent contractors," for the independent contractor himself his status does reduces taxes indirectly because of the ability to deduct from gross income all legitimate business expenses including personal and fringe benefits.

Of great importance, you should know that an independent contractor doing business as a corporation stands the lowest risk of being audited by the IRS. The major reason for this interesting statistic we explained a moment ago; the IRS is much more likely to audit a payor firm where it has the possibility of reclassifying as "employees" a large number of workers supposedly operating as "independent contractors." That approach gives the IRS lots of back taxes and penalties. An audit at the level of the payee/worker would catch only one worker in reclassification, a waste of time and energy from the IRS viewpoint.

Independent contractors, however, must pay ordinary income taxes, Federal Unemployment Tax Act (FUTA) taxes, and Social Security taxes in the form of the self-employment "Federal Insurance Contributions Act" (FICA) tax, which is about 2 to 3 percent less than the FICA tax a company employer would have to pay for an employee. (When a company pays FICA tax, part is borne by the company and part is deducted from the employee's wages.) Self-employed independent contractors also must estimate their individual income taxes for each year, then pay a quarter of the estimated amount owed to the federal and state governments each calendar quarter. Failure to pay or late payment means hefty penalties and interest added.

Independent contractors receive a Form 1099 at the end of the year. Like the W2, this form reports to the IRS the amounts paid, but in the case of the report on 1099 there is no tax withheld.

Form 1099 is required for payments over $600 per year, to individuals, partnerships, and other unincorporated entities. Certainly, receiving only one Form 1099 would bolster an IRS argument that an individual was an employee rather than an independent contractor -- so it is important to develop a variety of income sources (in addition to the good business sense of diversifying one's income).

There is no Form 1099 filed for payments to corporations, and as a practical matter this helps the incorporated independent contractor step aside from the entire independent contractor vs. employee debate. A corporation, by definition, cannot be an employee. And the fact that no Form 1099 even appears in the IRS computer next to the individual's name keeps one from even being swept into a random sampling of independent contractors for audit.

Becoming an Independent Contractor

If you structure your job properly you can convert an employer into a client and get paid more money for doing the same job as an independent contractor rather than an employee.

Once a worker converts to independent contractor status, the former employer no longer has a legal obligation to withhold and pay income, Social Security and unemployment taxes or workman's compensation benefits. This frees the company from the bookkeeping headaches of calculating, deducting and forwarding tax payments to the government, of processing paperwork for health and life insurance and of providing supplies and equipment.

Since a company can realize major savings under this new arrangement, a newly independent contractor should be able to negotiate increased pay benefits from some of those savings. Take into account the value of benefits such as sick leave, employee discounts, and health, disability, and life insurance.

This option should not be dismissed as some wild dream reserved for mavericks. Thousands more "mainstream" workers follow this new work route each year. House painters, floor layers, researchers, writers, custom seamstresses, management experts, engineers, carpenters, electricians, insurance claims processors, bookkeepers, and those in many other occupations successfully turn themselves into independent private contractors.

If you choose to operate as an unincorporated business, the "sole proprietorship" we have already discussed, you must pay all business expenses yourself, many of which may not be deductible against your personal income tax liability. The self-employment Social Security tax takes a big bite and is not deductible for an unincorporated business.

Top Ten Problems with a Home Office

If you don't incorporate and you do work at home, you may be able to benefit from the "home office" deduction, but the IRS is strict in applying rules as to what qualifies for a deduction in such cases. It became even more difficult to benefit from the home office deduction after a 1994 U.S. Supreme Court ruling that greatly tightened the definition of a "home office" for tax purposes.

The case involved a suburban Washington, D.C. anesthesiologist who worked at several hospitals but whose only "office" was at home where he did all his paperwork and billing. The Court held that the doctor's one room home office didn't qualify for a home office deduction because most of the time he was working elsewhere rather than at home. Prior to this unwelcome ruling, expenses related to the use of a home office would have been generally deductible against business income if the business owner had no other office and worked a substantial part of his or her time there.

Under the new rules the IRS says a home office qualifies only if it is used exclusively for business. If the kids watch TV in the same room, it's not an office for tax purposes. The IRS also makes a distinction about what constitutes a "principal office." For example, the IRS says a salesman who spends most of his time on the road visiting customers does meet their test of "substantial" use of his home as a "principal office." On the other hand, if the a person rarely ventures away from his home office and conducts his business by phone, mail and E-mail, the IRS says that's a bona fide home office.

Legislation now pending in Congress seeks to broaden the definition of a home office and remove inequities and confusion. These proposals would allow business owners who do most of their work outside their home, such as plumbers or salesmen, to claim the deduction so long as their home office serves as their business headquarters.

Since 1991 individuals claiming a home office have been required to fill out and file with their income tax a separate IRS Form 8829. About 1.5 million such forms are filed each year.

If your home office does qualify for IRS purposes, you can deduct costs of your home mortgage interest or rent, real estate taxes, insurance, home improvements and repairs that contribute to the upkeep of the office such as installing a home security system or fixing a heating or air conditioning system. One can also depreciate the part of a home used as an office. Expenses must be apportioned in percentages between home and office portions of the house, using an IRS square footage test.

If your home office expenses exceed your business income, you can carry forward the loss to next year's business income. Like every thing else involving the IRS, it is absolutely necessary to keep detailed records to support your deductions, especially is they challenge your home office status.

Wealth from Tax Deductions

One area of finance you will need to know about, in addition to building business equity, is how to create business wealth by deducting from taxable income legitimate business expenses, thereby reducing potential income tax liability and increasing profits.

Generally speaking, you can:

- convert your "personal" expenses into business tax-deductions;

- divide business income among several family members to avoid the full impact of progressive income tax rates on one individual;

- have your business compensate you with tax-free benefits in lieu of a larger, taxable personal salary;

- deduct vacation and travel costs under certain conditions;

- write off as a corporate business expenses the costs of establishing and operating your home office.

Conducting your own business as a corporation allows tax deductibility for many goods and services your company purchases, things you might otherwise purchase yourself using your own personal income. Goods and services you once were forced to buy with your own after-tax dollars suddenly become deductible expenses, in effect tax-free fringe benefits the business provides for its employees -- even if that's only you. One person corporations are permitted in almost every state; you need no other employees to take advantage of these tax breaks yourself.

Whether you have one or several employees, the federal tax treatment of corporate employee benefits is another advantage of incorporating your business. IRS rules recognize two general types of employee fringe benefits, those special benefits provided specifically for one employee, or those broader categories of benefits equally available to all workers within a given class.

Special Benefits

Among the specific benefits the law allows tax-free for employees that are tax-deductible as a business expense for a corporate employer are:

- Group accident and health insurance plans

- Group-term life insurance up to $50,000

- Group prepaid legal services

- Cafeteria or flexible-benefit meal plans

- Van-pooling transportation arrangements

- Scholarships and fellowships for training

- Dependent care assistance for workers with children

- Educational assistance related to an employee's job

General Benefits

Provision of **health and medical insurance** for employees offers a good example of the kinds of advantages that flow from incorporating your own business.

Once a worker no longer has group coverage available, an employee who leaves a larger company to start his or her own business often is shocked by the high-cost of individual health insurance premiums necessary to obtain comparable protection. A family plan with comprehensive coverage and dental benefits can cost an individual outside a group as much as $400 a month or more. But when that individual incorporates his own business, the new company can purchase health insurance and deduct the cost as a business expense.

What's even better for the recipient, health insurance benefits do not count as income for individual income tax purposes. The only major restriction on corporate health care insurance plans is that benefits must be equally available to all employees within certain groups as defined by IRS regulations.

Special health insurance or other company benefits are considered taxable income if availability is restricted only to officers or other highly compensated employees. This rule does not present a problem to a one-employee corporation, but benefit plans must be drafted so that future permanent full-time employees will be eligible for the same benefits.

Life insurance protection, tax-free for the covered employee and tax-deductible for the company, is another great benefit made possible by operating as a corporation. When a company creates a group term life insurance plan, covered employees receive the first $50,000 of coverage tax-free. The percentage of the company-paid life insurance premium for more than $50,000 of coverage is reportable as ordinary income by the insured worker, an amount determined by IRS tables taking into account age, years of service, compensation, and the employee's position in the company. The employer must be the owner of record of the insurance policy to qualify for deductibility.

One drawback is that life insurance coverage usually ends at an employee's retirement, although some retired persons need and want continued insurance which can be very costly if paid for by retired employees themselves.

A corporation has the ability to offer employees many other tax-free benefits, all cost-deductible for the company. For example, if an employer does not incur a substantial cost including lost revenue providing certain benefits, they can be given to workers tax-free, as when the boss allows waiters and other help to have free meals at a restaurant. As a general rule, to qualify as tax-free, such add-on employee benefits must be of the same nature the business provides to the public.

Qualified employee merchandise discounts are tax-free when they don't exceed the employer's gross profit margin on the product, or are more than 20 percent of the price charged to other customers.

Also among "fringe benefits," a business can provide certain goods or services tax-free that otherwise would be deductible trade or business expenses for the employee if he or she personally paid for them. Free parking for employees' motor vehicles on or near the business premises is considered such a fringe benefit. The employer can deduct the value of the parking provided, and the employee needn't count that value as taxable personal income.

Certain fringe benefits are tax-free if their value is so small ("de minimis") that accounting for them is unreasonable or impractical. Typing a personal letter on company time, company cocktail parties, picnics, and holiday gifts are all unreportable "de minimis" fringe benefits. For example, employee personal use of a copying machine is tax-free if the employer shows that 85 percent of the machine's use is for business.

THE CORPORATION

Centuries of professional and commercial experience in the United States have proven the corporation to be the best organization for American businesses. We have looked at corporations from the viewpoint of both the "employee" and the "independent contractor," now let's consider the corporation itself, its formation and operation, its advantages and disadvantages.

There are many good reasons to incorporate your business or profession, including:

- limiting personal liability for business activities;

- increasing benefits while reducing personal taxes by shifting expenses to the corporation;

- centralizing management and control of business affairs;

- making possible uncomplicated transfers of business interests and corporate ownership;

- the general ease of doing business.

The magic legal solution bestowing all these benefits (and many more) is the **corporation** -- an entity the United States Supreme Court has defined as "an artificial being, invisible, intangible and existing only in contemplation of law."

A more explicit definition is that a corporation is a legal entity or "person" composed of one or more natural persons who conduct its affairs, the existence of which, in the eyes of the law, is entirely separate and distinct from those human individuals who join together to compose the corporation.

However abstract the corporation may be in theory, its very real in fact and its recognition in law gives it great power. Much of the business and trade in the United States is conducted in the corporate form, ranging in size from giants like General Motors and AT&T, down to your local "mom and pop" gas station/convenience store.

For business and professional people, the first thought that comes to mind when "incorporating" is discussed is the legal principle known as **"limited liability."** Many people who know little about the law in general are familiar with the fact that individuals who form a corporation to conduct business legally insulate themselves personally -- and their real and personal property -- from any debts, lawsuits and other claims which arise against their incorporated business. Instead of being personally liable, except in rare instances, the law holds the "corporation" and its assets responsible for such claims -- not the individual people who manage and own that corporation as officers, directors and shareholders.

It is worth noting as a practical matter that the corporation is best suited for active business pursuits, as compared to more passive business such as investment or simply holding title to real estate or personal property. You should also know that the limited liability offered by a corporation does not shield individual owners and/or employees from liability for their own errors or omissions such as malpractice by doctors, lawyers or other professionals. Neither does it personally protect the employee whose injurious conduct is clearly outside the scope of his or her employment.

Since corporations are, as the Supreme Court said, entities "in contemplation of law," corporate formation, structure and powers are governed by the laws of each of the fifty states, the District of Columbia, Guam, the Virgin Islands and Puerto Rico, in any one of which you can create your company. There is no federal corporation law as such, although many years ago it was customary for Congress to enact special legislation "chartering" national corporations such as the American Legion or the Red Cross.

Individual corporation laws of the states and territories vary greatly; one state's law says the duration of a corporation's legal existence is 25 years, in another it is 99 years, in many it is "perpetual," meaning without limit in time. The law of the state in which you choose to incorporate will govern what your corporation can and cannot do. It is worth noting that in recent years changes in state corporation laws have tended to make all states similar in content, but there still are important differences which may be important to your business.

Some states have very liberal, flexible corporation laws allowing businesses more operating leeway than other states. Notable in this freer functioning category are Delaware and Nevada.

What A Corporation Can Do

According to government statistics, about 80 percent of America's small businesses are unincorporated. Considering the personal financial risks involved when a businessperson "goes naked," that's a surprising show of ignorance. Incorporating could reduce the income taxes of many of these businesses, but apparently their owners don't realize the corporation is America's best small-business tax shelter.

To understand how a corporation can save you money, we'll consider a typical example of a small retail business jointly owned by a husband and wife and operated as a sole proprietorship. The business has annual gross sales of over $415,000 with a net income of about $48,800. The owners also earn about $4,000 in interest and $1,200 in dividends.

Out of this income, they must pay federal self-employment income taxes of about $6,900. They also have personal medical expenses of almost $10,000 (somewhat above average, but not unusual in many families). Because the law allows them to deduct only the cost of those medical expenses that exceed 7.5 percent of their total adjusted gross income, they can include only $6,300 of their medical expenses in their itemized deductions. Their federal income taxes are about $3,800.

Now suppose this couple incorporates their business. Immediately their corporation can establish and pay for a medical-expense reimbursement plan (or a "group health insurance plan" as it is often called), which means the company now pays their medical expenses. These payments are tax-free to the owners and deductible by the corporation from its income as a business expense, which reduces its taxes.

Other expenditures, such as an automobile purchase, also can be paid for by the corporation. The value of the vehicle's personal use is included in the business owners' gross personal income, but the purchase expense is deductible for the corporation. The company buying a motor vehicle as a business expense produces a great saving, as compared to a purchase by the owners using their own after-tax personal income.

The owners also can draw salaries from the corporation, but they need to pay themselves far less than the $48,800 they received as sole proprietors, since their medical and other expenses now are paid by the corporation. They can reduce their salaries to about $35,000, thereby eliminating $2,110 in Social Security self-employment taxes, (familiarly known as "FICA," after the Federal Insurance Contributions Act which imposed this tax). Using their full standard income tax deduction and two personal exemptions cuts their taxable income to $22,850. Their federal income taxes for the year are now down to $3,428. Total tax savings from incorporating so far are about $2,500.

Eventually, this couple can have their corporation establish a pension fund and other benefit programs for them. They can also receive more tax-advantaged cash from the corporation by buying needed business assets with their own funds, then leasing the equipment back to the company. While a corporation's total taxable income up to $50,000 is taxed at a 15 percent rate, with a bit of judicious planning most small businesses can hold down total taxable income to zero and thus avoiding most taxes. Or the company can show a loss, which can be carried over to future tax years to limit profits and taxes.

Based on this kind of attractive arithmetic, it certainly doesn't require the proverbial "rocket scientist" to figure out the major advantages of doing business in the corporate form.

How to Incorporate Your Business

That's the term -- "incorporation" -- describing the process by which a corporation is formed under state law.

Like most things having to do with the law, you can hire a lawyer to set up a corporation, but that is guaranteed to be expensive. A far better method is to allow a professional incorporation service to handle all arrangements for a much more modest fee than any lawyer would charge.

First, assuming you know the purpose of your business, the choice of a company name is in order, since both purpose and name must be included in the **"articles of incorporation,"** a basic document required to be filed with the appropriate state agency -- and in each state the agency varies.

A professional incorporation service will assist you in preparing the articles, handle the filing on your behalf and take care of paying a nominal fee that must be paid when filing the completed papers with the state agency. Before filing, the professional service also will ascertain if your proposed corporate name is available for your use -- a check to make sure the name you chose is not similar to, or the same as another existing company name. Usually corporate registration will be with the office of the secretary of state, the corporation counsel, the department of revenue, the commerce department, or a state agency with some similar title.

The articles will state the names of the original incorporators (formerly three persons were required, but many states now permit single person incorporation), the purpose of the corporation, the directors' meeting requirements, the number and classes of shares authorized to be issued, the location of the office, name of the registered agent and other major details.

After the articles are filed and any initial annual corporate taxes are paid, the corporate existence becomes a matter of public record -- and your company is ready to do business.

What kinds of business, commercial or professional activity need the special protection afforded by operating in the corporate form?

The short answer is -- any activity where there exists potential liability. This protection is especially needed if you have one or more employees; if you frequently interact with the public, clients, patients, other businesses; if you are involved in joint ventures with others; engage in any hazardous activity; or, even if you just share office space or facilities with other professionals with whom you are not otherwise associated.

If you are currently acting on your own in any of these business situations, working unprotected as a sole proprietor, you could be just one law suit away from personal and family financial ruin.

Reasons for Incorporation

Asset protection is not the only good reason for formation of a business corporation. As we saw with the example of the couple who incorporated their business, you can also use a corporation to increase your available cash by reducing personal taxes to a bare minimum and having the corporation provide you with many benefits.

Operating a business in the corporate form allows company officers and directors to have the company finance many of their individual expenses. For example, as we pointed out in the example, you can create a corporate health and medical-expense plan entirely paid for by the company, tax deductible for the corporation as a business expense, with tax-free benefits to the employees included in the plan. The corporation can also pay for life insurance, pension and related benefits for officers and employees. Other necessary expenditures treated as legitimate business expenses include the purchase of automobiles, equipment and travel.

Depending on the nature of the exact benefit, all or part of the value of such goods and services given employees must be included in the recipient's gross income, but these are tax deductible business expenses for the corporation, thus reducing its net income and lowering company taxes. It is also less costly for an employee to include the value of the company benefit received in his or her gross income, rather than purchasing the same things with the employee's net after-tax personal disposable income.

In addition to health and pension benefits, tax breaks and limited personal liability, there are other solid reasons for incorporation:

- Ownership of corporate shares of stock is more easily transferable to family members as gifts or by sale to others, even by bequests at death. Stock transfers can be restricted in a closed corporation to a defined, limited group, when continued close private management control is an objectives.

- Since the corporation has a life of its own ("in perpetuity"), the death of officers or directors does not interrupt the business and their replacement by surviving directors is immediate.

- Many businesses give corporate discounts for goods and services, such as air and other travel, and these price breaks can add up to large savings for employees and company officers.

Many businesses find it useful to establish multiple corporations as a means of limiting liability and segregating the possibilities of claims against assets. For example, a transportation company might separately incorporate a company for the sole purpose of holding title to its motor vehicles, thus shielding other company assets from claims resulting from accidents.

Let The IRS Pay For Your New Home

Your home can, in a sense, be free to you for all the years you live in it. The key is to make your home a deductible expense.

If you buy a personal residence for $300,000 and are taxed at a 40% rate -- which many, if not most, people are -- you would have to earn at least $500,000 to pay for it. And that doesn't include a penny of interest on the mortgage (which is deductible). No matter how much you pay, your investment is worth whatever the property is worth -- which might be a lot less than you anticipated.

But suppose you could make the purchase a deductible expense? In some special situations, you can. If a business purchases a property for $300,000, and depreciates the expense over the mortgage period, the cost to the company would be only $300,000 rather than $500,000 -- a $200,000 savings. Remember, though, land is not depreciable -- to anyone.

Similarly, investment property may be depreciated (deducted over a period of years). Here again, the real cost of acquisition is greatly reduced.

The trick then is to turn residential property into business or investment property, thus allowing you to deduct the cost of acquisition and thereby save enough money to give you a new home free.

You cannot depreciate your primary residence. By definition, the place you live is a personal expense, not a business or investment expense. But if you buy another home, for investment purposes, you would be able to deduct the expenses, including the depreciation. Likewise, if you have a business of your own (this is just one of the many instances in which having a business can pay off), and the business needs a place to operate from, you can -- in certain cases -- have the business (especially if it is a corporation) buy a property and deduct the expenses. In this case, the business would buy a place from which to conduct business. And you would rent from the business a portion of the property as a living space.

This is the opposite of the typical "office in the home" situation...from a tax perspective. At the same time, it is precisely the same arrangement. But in this case, the property is business property, and as such, fully deductible. You just have to pay fair market rent for the part of the place you occupy. The value of the portion you occupy will be significantly depressed by the fact that you share the residence with a business. You can imagine how much less it would be worth to you if you had to share with such a business and adjust the rent accordingly.

The rent is not, of course, a business expense. It is a personal living expense and cannot be deducted. Still, the savings may be significant.

Your incorporated business buys a house (watch out for zoning and other regulatory problems) from which to conduct business. It pays $200,000 and deducts both the interest and the principal (as depreciation) over the life of the mortgage. Thus the total cost of acquisition is $200,000...before tax dollars. The house would rent for $1,500 a month. But since you have to share the property with a business...a fair market rent may be just $750, maybe even including utilities. Meanwhile, the business gets to deduct the maintenance, utilities, and other costs of operation.

The only taxable amounts involved are the monthly payments you make to the business in rent. And you have to watch out that you don't end up getting these amounts taxed twice, or even three times...by ending up with a profit in the company, which is taxed at the corporate rate, and then paying it out to you again...where it is taxed at your personal rate. You have to pay attention, in other words, to the details in a transaction like this.

How much can this arrangement save you? Let's say the mortgage payments are $2,000 per month for 20 years. You can only depreciate the improvements, not the lot, of course, but let's not make this example too complicated by assuming that the lot has minimal value. So you get to deduct the entire $200,000 purchase price over the 20-year period. (Be sure to check allowable depreciation schedules.) Plus, let's say upkeep and utilities average $200 per month...all deductible as well, for a deduction of another $48,000. This brings a total deductible amount of $248,000... which is a savings of $99,200 in taxes.

But, remember that we still have to pay the tax on the rent we pay. Alas, that amount works out to $72,000. So the net effect is a savings of a little more than $27,000.

However, the savings do not occur all at once. They're spread out over 20 years. Thus, the magic of compounding comes into play. Each year, you save about $1,350. With compounding at 10%...at the end of 20 years, you'd have $55,806. Here's another variation:

Your corporation can lease your land from you and build a house on it. You rent the house until it reverts to you at the expiration of the lease. The house can be in Hawaii...or the Upper East Side of New York City. The corporation depreciates the cost of construction and deducts the cost of maintaining the house.

The corporation's lease payments to you for the use of the land are deductible to the corporation. Your rental payments for the use of the house are income to the corporation.

When the land lease ends, say after 20 years, the land and building are both yours. You need not recognize any income as a result of the improvements the corporation made to your land. Your basis in the house will be zero, because you recognized no income.

If you sell the house, all proceeds will be long term capital gains. If you occupy the house as your residence and are qualified (over age 55, file a joint return with your spouse, and have lived in the house for three out of five years), you can take advantage of the one-time $125,000 exclusion. On the other hand, if you leave the property to your heirs, the value to them will be the fair market value at the time of your death, and the capital gains will never be taxed.

Now, having said all that, we hasten to add that any time you start to fool around with IRS regulations you run into problems. Basically, the IRS has the job of collecting money from people. And though it is well established that you have the right to organize your affairs in any way you please in an attempt to lower your tax liability, the IRS and Congress are determined to try to prevent you from exercising that right.

But for now, let us just point out that you need expert advice to set up a tax-avoiding structure such as the one we are explaining here. The specific form of the structure will depend on your own personal situation and your goals.

Now: let's add in the deductibility angle.

Many of the regions of opportunity are rural, farming areas. And there's a special angle in the tax law that could turn this into an important and powerful wealth-building tool.

Instead of buying a house, you buy a "farm." There's nothing that says a farm has to be big. It might only be a couple of acres. But to make this work, it has to be serious.

You lease the farm to your corporation. Your company will do the farming, just as the big agri-businesses do. Then your company figures it needs you on the scene to help do the farm work. So it makes you a deal. It builds you a new house...and you agree to live in it and attend to the farm chores. Guess what? Now the house is depreciable by the company -- meaning that the company can deduct it over time. The costs of maintaining the house are deductible currently. Even utility costs may be deductible.

And guess what else. You don't have to pay the corporation rent. That's the deal with the company. You didn't really want to live in the house. You're just doing it as a convenience to the company. That's why it's a deductible company expense...and not income to you.

And guess what else. After the lease expires on your land, what happens to the house? Does the company pick it up and move it off? No way. It wouldn't make economic sense. It leaves it where it was. You get it FREE. Wait until you see what this does to your bottom line!

You sold your $200,000 house. You bought the (farm) land for $20,000, let's say. You paid off the mortgage. You might have lent the other $80,000 to the corporation to build the house, but for the sake of avoiding too complicated a picture, let's just say the corporation put up its own money or got it elsewhere. In any event, since the house is deductible to the corporation (presumably over the term of the lease), here's what happens.

Each year, the company deducts a part of the $80,000. Let's say we can get away with depreciating the property over 15 years -- saying that is the term of the lease. It makes economic sense (which doesn't mean it will actually fly, of course).

What happens is that each year the company deducts the 1/15th of $80,000. At a 40% tax rate, this deduction is worth $2,133 in extra cash. This amount can then be invested and compounds along with the other wealth-building components in this example. In 10 years, with compounding, you have $37,373. Plus, you have the house...or you will have it when the lease expires.

Can you really do this? Yes...but. In a similar case, the court has ruled that you could. Remember, however, these cases tend to turn on the details. Make sure you do it right.

Altogether so far, we've shown you how to get rid of the house in the suburbs and get a new house in a better area. This change alone could add a total of over $200,000 to your bottom line...the combined effect of eliminating your mortgage... owning a home that is rising in value...deducting the cost of the home...and getting the home for FREE at the expiration of the lease...

...and we still have not factored in the money you save from deducting the expense of utilities and maintenance. Suppose that cost is just $200 per month and that you pay taxes at a total rate of about 40%. Further suppose that you invest the savings (about $1,400 a year) at 10%. The bottom line of all this is an additional $25,000 or so.

Rent Your Home To Your Corporation For A Double Tax Break

If you don't have your corporation own your home, there is still another way to draw some tax-free cash from your business. Rent your home to your corporation. In general, you won't pay any tax on the rental income, and your company will get a business deduction for the rental payments.

If you do business as a corporation, you can get the same double tax break for setting up a home office. A convenient loophole in the tax law gives you a chance to generate enough passive income to offset passive losses.

Instead of going to a hotel for your next conference or shareholder meeting, rent out your home. As long as you rent it for less than 15 days a year, you don't have to pay taxes on rental income. And as long as you follow some basic rules, your company can deduct the rental payments. Just charge a reasonable amount of rent and make sure there's a bona fide business purpose for the use of your home. Find out what a hotel would have charged for sleeping and meeting rooms, then bill that amount to your company. That way, the

IRS won't question the deduction, even though the rental isn't an arms length transaction.

Most taxpayers take advantage of the 15-day rule only when they rent out their vacation homes, but the rule applies to your principal residence too. That's not all. Keep in mind that for tax purposes, boats and motor homes are also considered dwelling units as long as they have plumbing, kitchens, sleeping quarters, and living rooms. If you're already taking mortgage interest deductions on your boat as a second residence, you can host a business cruise on your boat and have the IRS pick up the tab.

If you have unused passive losses, you can work an even better deal with your corporation...

Basically, income from tangible property rented to a corporation in which you have an interest is considered passive income. But thanks to a loophole that Congress unwittingly opened in the 1986 tax law, you might have more passive income than you realized to soak up your passive losses.

Here's what happened. The 1986 tax law stopped the practice of deducting passive losses against regular (nonpassive) income. But the IRS still feared that corporation owners who rent property to their companies would take too many deductions up front. So Congress changed the 1986 law. Now it says you can deduct only mortgage interest, property taxes, and casualty losses from the rental income you get from your company. You can no longer deduct other expenses, like maintenance and repairs. But that means you'll have more rental income that isn't reduced by expenses. And the more rental income you have, the more passive losses you can deduct.

Ideally, you can charge your corporation rent for setting up an office in your home. The only restrictions are that you must charge a fair market rental rate and provide a business service to your firm. (For instance, renting out storage space wouldn't qualify.) As a result, your company deducts the rental payments, and you get tax free rental income by deducting your passive losses.

Don't try this with a Subchapter-S corporation, a partnership, or a joint venture. In such cases, the rental payments are considered regular income.

Subchapter "S" Corporations

One problem created by using the corporate form is **"double taxation"** -- first, by imposition of federal and states income taxes on corporate income, then by the federal and state personal income tax levied on the dividends paid to shareholders of the company, as well as salaries and on other company payments to officers and directors. Admittedly unusual, federal law provides relief from this double taxation problem, in an effort to promote small businesses.

A section of the IRS Code known as **Subchapter "S"** allows a small business corporation to elect to have the undistributed taxable income of the corporation taxed as personal income for the shareholders, thus avoiding payment of any corporate income tax.

Under the Subchapter "S" election, if your minor children are made company shareholders, this spreads the company wealth among all family shareholders, reducing individual personal income tax liability. This means lower income taxes for everyone, adults included. The other side of that coin is that corporate losses can also be claimed directly by the shareholders against their personal tax liability. In this tax-saving sense, the Subchapter "S" tax status is like that of a general partnership, but it provides the corporate personal liability protection a partnership does not enjoy.

A small business corporation can qualify for Subchapter "S" treatment if:

- it is properly incorporated under state law;
- has 35, or fewer shareholders;
- has only one class of stock;

- has shareholders who qualify as IRS-recognized individuals, estates or trusts, (other share holding corporations or partnerships do not qualify);

- is not "affiliated" with another corporation, meaning it does not hold 80 percent or more ownership of another corporation.

Corporate Structure

Corporations have the advantage of a defined centralized management structure with consolidated control, flexibility and permanency -- as well as limited liability for shareholders. Corporate powers are so comprehensive they are almost co-extensive with the powers a human individual can exercise in a business.

The owners of a corporation are the shareholders who own stock in the company; the board of directors manage the business; the officers -- president, vice president, secretary and treasurer -- are responsible for day-to-day operation. Most state laws minimally require the basic corporate structure just described.

Be aware that if state law allows, small corporations, often called "close" or "closely held" corporations, can operate with only one or two stockholders, directors and officers, several or all of whom may be the same person. Many states like Delaware, New York and Nevada, allow one-person corporations with the same person serving in all of the required capacities.

At first glance this may seem complicated, but the minimum requirement of only one corporate officer/director/ shareholder is just a matter of routine "paper work" which a professional incorporation service can handle in order to meet the requirements of state law.

Understand what this means; an individual doing business can easily and quickly convert him or herself into corporation status with all the benefits and protections that entails, and that person then exercises all the powers the company operation requires.

A "stock corporation" is a company that issues shares of capital stock, title to which is held by the shareholders making them the owners of the corporation. State law authorizes a stock company to pay profits to the shareholders in the form of dividends. Generally, stock corporations, shares of which are not listed or traded on a public stock exchange, are called "closely held" or "privately owned" or "close corporations," and they are usually exempt from federal laws controlling the issuance and registration of publicly offered and sold securities that are listed on public stock exchanges.

Organization and Operation

Regardless of the number of directors, one or more, once the state officially recognizes your corporation, the first essential step is to hold an organizational meeting to elect the board of directors and officers, adopt bylaws, set the price or initial stock values, approve contracts of employment and other start-up authorizations, such as opening a company bank account.

The board of directors is required to meet at least once a year for election of officers and directors and other business. Full and accurate minutes of all meetings and the business transacted must be kept, both to satisfy the law and protect the corporate status. Failure to keep such records can result in state revocation of the corporate charter and worse, faulty record keeping can produce personal liability for officers, directors and shareholders. Record keeping is important because in one sense, the company records are the only tangible evidence of the corporate existence.

Keeping records means just what it says; there must be written corporate by-laws and regular directors meetings with minutes keep in a record book showing all authorizations for company actions including loans, major purchases, and adoption of plans such as employee health and insurance programs. There should be a corporate stock ledger book showing all current stockholders names, addresses and number of shares owned. There should also be a separate company bank account that keeps apart any personal funds or transaction of the business owners or directors.

Like other legal entities, corporations have the power to hold title to property, enter into contracts, sue and be sued, and to do all things necessary to carry on business. Corporations exist in perpetuity, or until they are formally dissolved by either the act of the directors, or by the state -- the latter usually occurs after failure to pay annual state operating fees, taxes or to file required reports.

Since your company is likely to be a "closely-held" corporation, it is important you make clear to the general public and to creditors that they are dealing with a corporation -- not with you personally. Failure to make known the use of the corporate business form can result in a loss of limited liability protection for individual officers and directors, negating the whole purpose of incorporation.

Most state laws require a company name to include words notifying the public of the corporate form, such as "inc." -- incorporated; "corp." -- corporation; "ltd." -- limited; "co." -- company; or variations of those words.

Use of corporate checking accounts, stationery, business cards and documents (always signed in a corporate capacity), will protect you and the company -- and allow people to easily understand they are doing business with a corporation, not an individual acting under a trade or company name.

Maintaining corporate identity is especially important when obtaining financing for a new business which often requires personal guarantees for loans, unless the corporation is well capitalized. All loan documents should clearly reflect whether it is the corporation or the individual who is primarily responsible for repayment. Officers should always indicate their official company position when signing on its behalf, following their name with the correct corporate title, or adding a phrase such as "For the XYZ Co., Inc."

Piercing the Corporate Veil

Officers, directors and controlling shareholders have a general fiduciary duty of loyalty and care which should govern all their corporate conduct. Unless they breach that duty by gross negligence or acts in bad faith, they usually will have no personal liability to third parties. Third parties have to show personal wrongful conduct on the part of a company official or director to hold them personally responsible, extra-corporate actions which would support application of the legal doctrine known as **"piercing the corporate veil**."

It is indeed possible to breach the wall of personal liability provided by incorporation, and for your asset safety you should know how such exceptions can occur.

Certain acts of directors and officers may be grounds for a company creditor to ask a court to "pierce the corporate veil" -- which means just what it says. For example, if the corporation cannot pay a creditor's proven debt or a court judgment claim, the individuals who own and manage the corporation can be held personally responsible for company obligations, even though they have given no previous personal guarantees.

Personal liability can happen when:

- corporate debt is knowingly incurred when the company is already insolvent;

- required annual shareholders or board of directors meetings are not held, or other corporate formalities are not observed;

- corporate records, especially minutes of directors meetings, are not properly or adequately maintained;

- shareholders remove unreasonable amounts of funds from the corporation, endangering its financial stability;

- there is a pattern of consistent non-payment of dividends, or payment of excessive dividends;

- there is a general commingling of corporate activity and/or funds and those of the person or persons who control the corporation;

- there is a failure to maintain separate offices, the company has little or no other business and is only a facade for the activities of the dominant shareholder who is in fact, the corporate "alter ego."

In order to maintain personal limited liability, it is essential these described actions be avoided. Courts in recent years have found ever expanding reasons to hold directors, officials and shareholders personally liable for corporate responsibilities. Among other activities courts have found that may impose personal liability are improper corporate guarantees of loans or contracts benefitting an officer, timing of the sale of a controlling interest in the company for self-benefit, profiting from inside information, transactions with other businesses which may constitute conflicts of interest, unreasonable loans to company officials, and extension of unwarranted credit.

Directors are generally held to a higher standard of duty than officers because acting as a board, they hold the ultimate controlling power, including the election or removal of officers.

The IRS has no need to "pierce the corporate veil," because under federal law, directors and officers can be held liable for federal taxes owed by the corporation -- both corporate income taxes on annual business net profit and for unpaid payroll taxes withheld for employees. In fact the owner/manager of a corporation can be held personally liable to the IRS for all unpaid payroll taxes, plus a 100 percent penalty.

As an extra layer of personal asset protection, experts recommend that in a closely held family corporation, only one spouse, either husband or wife, serve as a director -- thus limiting potential family liability in the event the corporate veil is pierced by adverse legal action.

State of Incorporation

If your corporation is intended as an operating business in a specific state, usually the one in which you live, or in which you intend to locate and do business, that usually is the best state in which to incorporate.

A company doing business in more than one state will be required to "qualify to do business" in states other than the one in which it is originally incorporated. This means formally registering in other states, paying an additional franchise or other initial tax, filing annual reports and paying annual taxes in those states -- all because yours is a "foreign corporation," chartered in another state. In other words, government red tape is multiplied by incorporation in one state and doing business in another. If you plan a multi-state business operation, all these legal formalities in each state also can be provided by a professional incorporation service.

If you have a multi-state business operation, "qualifying to do business" in other states is an acceptable burden, but if interstate business is not likely, your company initially should be incorporated in the state in which you are located and doing business. Your corporation can always qualify later in other states if business expands across state lines.

Delaware and Nevada

Many Americans have heard that the small east coast state of Delaware is the place to incorporate a business. If, as we have said, you intend to conduct a multi-state business,

Delaware may well be the jurisdiction in which to consider your incorporation.

That's because the corporation laws of Delaware have been tailored by the state legislature to fit the needs of businesses, large and small. Not only are Delaware corporation fees low, but its corporation laws are liberal, flexible and impose only minimal requirements on a business wherever it may be located physically.

There's also the advantages and certainty that flows from decades of Delaware pro-management judicial decisions defining the meaning of almost every aspect of business law.

The state requires no minimal capital investment, while many other states require at least an investment of $500 or $1,000 to start. Delaware allows an anonymous one-person incorporation process that can be achieved by fax, phone or mail without ever having to visit the state. The state does not tax Delaware corporations that conduct no business in the state. Annual franchise fees are as low as $50.00 in most cases. Stock in Delaware companies owned by people outside the state is also income and estate tax free. Stockholders and directors can operate by unanimous consent in lieu of formal meetings and dividends can be paid out of profits as well as surplus.

In other words, Delaware makes corporate life easy for business because it depends on attracting and holding a high volume of businesses that produce major revenues for the state, second only to the state income tax.

At one time Delaware corporation laws were the most liberal in the nation, allowing great flexibility in business operation. This was particularly valuable to major corporations with thousands of stockholders all over the country and the world. That's why so many "Fortune 500" companies call Delaware their corporate home.

But for small, closely-held or family businesses, these powers are essentially meaningless since they don't need them. then too, many other states have liberalized their own laws in order to compete with Delaware and keep their local business at home.

Nevada, for example, is even more liberal than Delaware in both taxes and corporation laws and has great popularity these days among businesses.

Tax Savings In Nevada

Nevada is one of several states that have no corporate income tax, no state personal income tax and no corporate franchise tax.

Many large corporations use Nevada for warehousing because there is no inventory tax. That may seem beyond the reach of your small company, but if you organize all or part of your business as a Nevada corporation, you can contract with a local warehousing and fulfillment service to process and ship orders from Nevada.

Already such companies as Citibank and Porsche North America have moved their corporate headquarters to Nevada. For as little as $2,500 in corporate start-up fees, you can enjoy the same advantages as these corporate giants.

One of the major reasons for Nevada incorporation is the absence of a state income tax. If you live and do business in a high-tax state this can be the crucial factor. In California, for example, corporations pay a minimum of $9,600 on every $100,000 of taxable income.

If minimizing taxes is your concern, the strategy is to form a Nevada corporation and allow profits to accumulate there rather than in the high tax state in which you presently do business.

This is not difficult to accomplish. Suppose you have a small business with a major element of production or service that can be handled from Nevada. Locating a successful service corporation in Nevada means carefully avoiding rendering that service in a high-tax state. To do otherwise would subject the Nevada corporation to the high-tax state jurisdiction where it would have to pay. But a sales representative who travels a ten-state area can work for a Nevada distributor servicing those western states, paying salary and expenses out of the Nevada corporation and retaining sufficient commission to keep most of the profits in Nevada instead of the higher-tax state in which the rest of business is physically headquartered.

A company in a high-tax state can contract for sales management services from a Nevada corporation, paying that company a fixed fee in return for its employing your salesmen. Current employees can be switched to the new Nevada employer at the same salary and doing the same job. The only difference is the source of the paycheck.

The Nevada sales management company fee reasonably might be set at $75,000, a cool $47,000 more in management fees than your salesman's previously salary, meaning suddenly any net profit on his operation is cut to zero. That's good news because wiping out profit means no corporate income tax will be imposed in your own high-tax jurisdiction. Your Nevada corporate net profit is a non-taxable $47,000 and it's perfectly legal, so long as the invoicing, accounting and management of the sales activity is actually done by the Nevada corporation.

Transferring income and profit from high-tax jurisdictions to low-tax states is now common, and it works for any business sales or services other than those of a purely local nature.

Nevada corporate tax savings make incorporation there worth considering even if you have never incorporated before. Attractive tax benefits have spawned a whole new Nevada-based service industry to assist incorporation in that state. These are only corporate formation agents, not lawyers or accountants and any Nevada lawyer or accountant can perform the same service and render professional advice as well.

The most common pitfall in using a Nevada corporation is the temptation to cut corners, ignoring legal requirements. Unless all legal technicalities are strictly observed, directors meetings held, records kept, a company stands to lose not only tax savings, but the many other corporate protections offered under Nevada's liberal laws.

A professional incorporation service will be pleased to form your corporation in Delaware, Nevada, your home state or any other state you choose.

Other Tax Havens In The United States

You should be aware that although the federal tax is the same everywhere, state income taxes vary considerably. Some states, such as Nevada and Wyoming, have no income tax at all, and for certain types of businesses, you may be able to base in one of those tax havens. State tax laws change frequently, and it is important to obtain current advice from a tax professional.

Manufacturing businesses, and some service businesses, in Puerto Rico receive income tax exemptions for up to ten years, but are within the customs territory of the United States, so there is no duty on selling your goods on the mainland. Traveling between Puerto Rico and the mainland is just like traveling between states. Almost all of the world's largest pharmaceutical companies now have their factories for the American market in Puerto Rico. Puerto Rico is the only place in the United States that is exempt from federal income taxes -- it is not part of the U.S. for income tax purposes.

Puerto Rico income tax law also exempts dividends and capital gains from the shares of companies that have been granted a tax holiday. A U.S. citizen who resides for the entire calendar year in Puerto Rico does not pay federal income tax, but normally pays Puerto Rican income tax on his worldwide income. But since the dividends and capital gains from these tax holiday companies are exempt because of the Puerto Rican tax incentive laws to attract business, you can accumulate your profits, and then spend a year in Puerto Rico. During that year you pay out a huge dividend or sell the company. The money will not be subject to either Puerto Rican or federal income taxes. But be sure you have established your legal residence in Puerto Rico -- well documented with a lease or house purchase -- by December 31st of the preceding year and maintain it until at least January 2nd of the following year.

Using a Professional Incorporation Service

We have repeatedly emphasized the value of doing business in the corporate form. Equally important has been our underscoring of the fact that all corporations must meet legal requirements at the time of incorporation and during their existence in order to protect their privileged status.

This means that when you decided to incorporate, you must have it done right, and later, when the business is up and running, all legal formalities must continuously taken care of on a timely basis.

Experience shows that the best way to accomplish these objectives is to have incorporation done by an incorporation service, professionals who know their business and the law and who charge a lot less than attorneys would demand for the same services. Not only to they not charge legal fees, you pay far less for normal ongoing service, including annual statutory renewal requirements.

The service will file your incorporation application in the state you designate, file with the IRS and obtain your Employer Identification Number (EIN), file the IRS form allowing you to operate as a Subchapter "S" company, and pay any sales tax or other incorporation fees the state requires. In addition, the service will provide you with a complete incorporation kit containing printed minutes, stock certificates and a corporate seal.

If you wish, the service will also act as your registered agent in the state of your choice, an important legal agency required by law for service of process on your company.

For information on a highly-recommended national service that can form a corporation for you in any state, write to:

INC PLAN USA
Attn: Incorporation Information Package
Trolley Square, Suite 26-C
Wilmington DE 19806

or telephone (800) 462-4633 or fax (302) 428 1274 (marking your fax "Attn: Incorporation Information Package").

THE WEALTH ACCUMULATION TRUST: YOU DON'T HAVE TO LEAVE THE COUNTRY TO FIND A TAX HAVEN

What Is a "CRT"?

This chapter will acquaint you with the near magical possibilities of a tax-saving, income-producing legal device known as a **"charitable remainder trust"** or **"CRT."** Although "CRT" is the currently popular term, these trusts are also known as "life income" and "wealth accumulation" trusts. Both descriptions are accurate - and therein lies the money magic.

A CRT is just the thing for a person seeking to avoid capital gains taxes on appreciated property, or in pursuit of increased retirement income or estate tax relief. But this trust is also the perfect vehicle to achieve your personal philanthropic goals, while also helping yourself and your family. In fact, while tax savings and income enhancement are central attractions of the CRT, the chief motivation should be the donor's charitable intentions. After all, when the final distribution of the trust assets is made - and they can be of considerable value - the charity of your choice will be the major beneficiary.

And in the meantime, there is no reason why the objects of your generosity cannot reward their benefactor with a seat on your church board of trustees, or your alma mater's establishment of a scholarship bearing your name.

What It Can Do for You:

So, let's consider just what the creation of a CRT can accomplish for **you.** Properly drafted, formulated and managed, a charitable remainder trust is an excellent "transfer tax" avoidance instrumentality that can -

- avoid completely any capital gains tax payment on your appreciated property, regardless of the original cost basis;

- convert your low-yield property into a high income investment guaranteed to provide you and your spouse the financial security of lifetime income, immediate or deferred, with greatly reduced income tax consequences;

- serve as a vehicle to receive the "roll over" of your qualified pension plan or Individual Retirement Account (IRA), increasing both retirement income andtax savings;

- provide you with an immediate substantial charitable income tax deduction against your taxes for the year in which the CRT is created;

- diminish estate and inheritance taxes on that property - and avoid the probate mess as well; and

- allow a greatly increased inheritance for your heirs, financed by the tax savings and increased income your CRT will provide.

Sounds too good to be true - or to be legal in present day, tax-oppressed America?

Read on; first about "trusts" in general for a little background course, then about CRTs in all their legal glory.

A point to keep in mind as you refresh your knowledge about trusts - a charitable remainder trust is what is known in the law as an **irrevocable living trust**," a concept we will explain in detail.

"Trust Me" - A Word About Trusts:

In life we often hear the word "trust" employed, almost always with a special, distinctive connotation. Invoking the Deity, "In God We Trust" is the official national motto etched on all U.S. currency and coinage. When people speak of "trust," they usually describe a unique personal relationship on which reliance rightfully can be placed. In the eyes of the law, the meaning of the word "trust" also partakes of this special quality of high purpose, reliance and mutual confidence.

In the law, a "**trust**" is a legal device in contract form allowing title to, and possession of property to be held, used and/or managed by one person, the **trustee**, or property manager, for the benefit of one or more other persons, the **beneficiaries**, or recipients. A trust is initiated by a **grantor**, or creator, the original owner of property that is transferred to the trust and becomes trust assets. In essence the contract, in the form of a "trust declaration," is between the grantor and the trustee, with the beneficiaries as third parties who profit from this voluntary arrangement.

A trust is one of the most ancient and flexible legal mechanisms available, and is useful for almost any purpose that is legal or not against public policy; a trust can conduct a business; hold title to and invest in real estate, cash, stocks, bonds, negotiable instruments and personal property; care for minors or the elderly; pay medical, educational or other expenses; provide financial support in retirement, marriage or divorce; and serve as a major avenue of avoidance for the muddle of probate courts and the burden of inheritance taxes.

By their very nature trusts are relatively complex and technical, a domain of lawyers and accountants, investment planners and bankers, which means expense of creation and administration. But do not let complexity or cost dampen your interest - a trust can play a major role in your estate, tax, gift and investment planning - and save (and make) you and your family lots of money - far more than it will cost to establish and operate.

Trust Creation:

In the usual situation, the person who creates a trust (variously called the "donor," "**grantor**" or "settlor") conveys legal title "in trust" to a body of his or her real or personal property or money (the "**corpus**") to a third party, (the "**trustee**"), perhaps a close friend, professional financial manager or a bank trust department, to be managed or invested by that trustee for the benefit of a named person or persons, the "**beneficiary**." Thus the burdens of property ownership and management fall to the trustee, while the benefits go to others, the beneficiaries.

The act of trust creation immediately transfers the legal title and absolute ownership of the trust property or "corpus" from the grantor to the trust. Assuming there is no fraudulent intent, this means the grantor's creditors cannot reach the transferred assets. Control of these trust assets henceforth is vested in the trustee, so long as the trust exists. The trustee's powers and duties can be broad or narrow, according to the terms of the trust declaration, the basic "master plan" authorizing and creating the trust, but they should carefully reflect the grantor's intentions as to how the objectives of the trust are to be achieved and how it is to operate.

The grantor may also be the trustee, or one of the trustees, but such an arrangement imposes a strict duty against self-dealing and conflict of interest, lest the validity of the trust itself be called into question by creditors, tax authorities or the courts. In almost every instance it is better to avoid potential legal challenges by not having the trust grantor act as trustee. This appropriate distance between grantor and trust is not absolute, since the grantor can retain the right to designate or change the trustee at will. The grantor may also be a beneficiary of the trust.

Trust beneficiaries receives only an equitable title to the income or assets of the trust, but this allows them to seek judicial intervention as a matter of right if there is reason to believe the trust is being administered improperly or the assets dissipated.

Trusts Come in Many Forms:

There are numerous specific types of trusts, each type characterized by different objectives and variables in the trust declaration terms, each with its own advantages, problems and tax results. At various stages of a person's economic life, one or more types of trusts may be appropriate, and as circumstances change, new ones might well be needed.

Perhaps the most common use of trusts occurs in **estate planning** where a trust can serve as an effective way to pass title to property, while avoiding lengthy and complicated probate court procedures and confiscatory inheritance taxes when the property owner dies. Nationally, in the United States, probate fees alone (exclusive of federal and state death taxes), average from one to 15 percent of the gross value of the entire estate, a enormous sum in many cases - and that much less for the heirs. The time-consuming probate process in some states, such as California, can require up to two years to complete.

A trust once established, especially if operative for a reasonable period of time, is less likely to be challenged in court as compared to a will which is far more susceptible to a contest during probate. The existence of a previously created trust is evidence of the grantor's sound mind and careful planning, an obvious defense to the charge of mental incompetency, often the basis for attacking the validity of a will, especially one written late in life.

The Living Trust:

A large number of trusts are created in the last will and testament (a "**testamentary trust**") of a deceased person, usually with the objective of providing for a spouse and heirs. This is a traditional use of the trust, but its popularity overlooks the great advantages of a **living trust**, one created while the grantor is still alive.

In order to create a trust other than by a will, the grantor must sign a written "**declaration**" or "indenture" which gives specific details of the trust objectives, operation and income distribution, both during the grantor's life and afterward. The declaration is the charter for all the trust purposes, powers and procedures, and as such, the drafting and content of this basic document is of the utmost importance.

Among other things, the trust declaration should define how the trustee is to invest the property, provide instructions for payment or accumulation of income earned by the trust, name and define the rights and benefits of the beneficiaries, set a duration for trust existence and distribution of property when it is to end, and define the relationship of the grantor to the trust and the trustee.

Decades of federal and state judicial decisions and U.S. Internal Revenue Service rulings interpreting trust documents by now have given every phrase special meaning, therefore the writing of the trust declaration requires expert advice, assistance and coordination. This is especially true because to be successful, a trust must be integrated fully with all other estate planning and legal arrangements the grantor may make.

A **living trust** is just what the term suggests; a trust created while the grantor is alive, also known as an "**inter vivos** trust." In contrast to the delayed establishment of a testamentary trust, a living trust is created by the grantor to take effect and operate immediately.

Typically a living trust provides for income for the beneficiaries during their lives, usually a grantor husband and his wife, and the disposition of the trust assets at the grantor's death, customarily to their heirs. The major benefit in a simple living trust is that upon the grantor's death, or the later death of the surviving spouse, trust assets avoid probate completely, title passing immediately to the named beneficiaries. There are also the secondary benefits of lifetime income and asset protection which a trust affords.

In creating a **revocable** living trust, a grantor voluntarily transfers title to his or her assets, but with a "string" attached. When a trust is "revocable," the grantor retains power during his or her lifetime to vary the trust terms, withdraw assets, or even end the trust entirely by formal revocation. Such a trust offers only limited asset protection, especially if the grantor is also the beneficiary during life, a cozy arrangement often challenged successfully by creditors.

Irrevocable Living Trusts:

A living trust also may be expressly created as **irrevocable**, denying a grantor the ultimate control, once the trust is created, over the transferred trust assets.

As a protection against asset attachment by the grantor's creditors, this is virtually perfect because the grantor no longer holds title to the property nor has ability to re-acquire it. The only possibility of successful attack by creditors might occur if the transfer can be proven to be fraudulent in some way.

Irrevocability is the unique feature of this type of trust, and a court finding irrevocability will usually shield trust assets from the grantor's creditors. But irrevocability is also the major disadvantage - if the grantor's circumstances change, the trust cannot be changed to meet them.

Under the law, the income and assets of a revocable or irrevocable trust are subject at least to one-time state and federal death taxes at the grantor's death. The trust property is included in the grantor's gross estate for tax purposes.

This means the fair market value of all estate assets above $600,000 - the federal estate tax exemption amount - are taxed on a 1994 scale of from 37 percent up to 60 percent, the exact tax percentage depending on the total size of the deceased's taxable estate, payable within nine months after death. But importantly, trusts can be arranged so that upon the subsequent deaths of named beneficiaries or their heirs, further death taxes are avoided, a savings for the eventual trust beneficiaries, although this helpful aspect is often remote in time.

When you consider the estimate that between now and the year 2020, personal estates valued in excess of ten trillion (with a "t") dollars ($10,000,000,000,000.00) are projected to pass to heirs, you realize the enormity of the need to avoid estate taxes as much as possible. We will talk more about this in a moment.

Taxes - Tools of Government Policy:

The United States Congress, and the legislatures of the several states, have a long history of employing taxation as a means to achieve certain perceived political, social and even religious objectives. Our legislators may have learned this tactic from the British Crown, whose unjust taxes on colonial American tea and documentary stamps, among other things, spawned a highly successful revolution, the concentric effects of which are still reverberating in the modern world.

Thus we Americans revel in "sin taxes" that boost the price of tobacco and alcohol products far beyond any intrinsic value a pack of cigarettes or a fifth of bourbon has in and of itself - even taking into account personal taste or addiction.

Thus the most valuable real estate in America, worth a combined total of billions of dollars, often located in the heart of major cities, is totally tax-exempt because it is owned, not by the Japanese, but by a recognized established religion - Protestant, Catholic or Jewish or whatever.

Before international free trade became a more acceptable political doctrine, almost all federal revenues came from heavy import taxes ("customs duties") on products and commodities, surely a revenue source but equally a means of protecting home-grown U.S. merchandise.

At times legislators have gone too far in the realm of social policy by taxation. In 1994 the U.S. Supreme Court ruled unconstitutional a Montana tax imposed on persons convicted of possessing, selling, distributing or manufacturing "controlled dangerous substances" - illicit drugs like marijuana or cocaine. The Court said such acts could be made punishable crimes, but that to impose additional tax liability amounting to millions of dollars based on the amount of drugs involved, in effect constituted double jeopardy and cruel and unusual punishment.

So revenue alone has never been the sole object of government tax laws.

Unquestionably the single greatest political, economic and social impact ever imposed by taxation in America began on February 25, 1913, the date the requisite number of states ratified the Sixteenth Amendment to the United States Constitution - giving Congress "the power to lay and collect taxes on incomes, from whatever source derived . . ." Many would argue it has been down hill ever since.

Fortunately, in 1913 when the income tax was authorized, Americans still firmly believed in those voluntary non-governmental institutions which had an admirable record of serving the needs of less fortunate citizens - thousands of voluntary religious, charitable, and philanthropic organizations and groups. In the days before the "welfare state" mentality took hold, these altruistic activities ranged from local soup kitchens to the vast eleemosynary exertions of men like Andrew J. Carnegie, a self-made Scottish-American steel baron who donated millions of dollars to build and support free public libraries, the International Endowment for World Peace and countless other causes.

Also fortunately - for those seeking legal ways by which to escape the ultimate excesses of modern federal income taxes - from 1913 on, Congress took into account the need for private philanthropy, writing federal tax law so as to promote charitable giving by individuals as well as organized groups. The original tax code contained then, as it does today, "tax breaks" for those willing to give of their personal substance to help their fellow man (and woman). Born in tandem with the federal income tax was the charitable tax deduction.

Under current law charitable deductions are available for donations to corporations organized or exclusively operated for religious, charitable, scientific, literary, or educational purposes, or for groups that foster the arts, sports competition, prevention of cruelty to children or animals, or to fraternal associations and veterans organizations.[1]

The Charitable Remainder Trust:

Prefaced by that short historical review, we turn to consideration of the **charitable remainder trust** - the **CRT**, a congressionally approved statutory device allowing those people of wealth who wish to "do good" - to do very well indeed. As you will see, it is no wonder the CRT has such wide popularity among the tax paying cognoscenti.

The CRT is a tax-exempt irrevocable living trust with one or more living income beneficiaries, and one or more qualified tax-exempt charitable remaindermen.[2] And remember "irrevocable" means what it says: the transferred property is no longer yours. As a general rule, most experts offer the opinion that for feasible operation, a CRT should start with assets worth at least $50,000; but others say as little as $20,000 is financially sound if the donor is young and the term of years for the trust is long, or if high-yield investments such as a mutual fund are pursued.

Although the discussion here centers on living charitable remainder trusts, a CRT also can be created in a last will and testament. A "testamentary CRT" is relatively rare, with a testator directing that a named percentage of the value of the trust be paid to the beneficiary for life, with the remainder afterward going to a qualified charitable organization. This arrangement allows the present value of the charity's deferred interest to be deducted from federal estate taxes.

The single most distinctive characteristic of the CRT, and the key to its associated tax and income benefits, is found in the identity of the ultimate beneficiary of the trust - the "remainderman", to use the quaint English common law term. When a CRT has fulfilled its terms, run its legal course, and is ready to go out of business, the law says the remaining assets ("the charitable remainder") must go to a "qualified" tax-exempt charitable organization as defined by the Internal Revenue Code.[3]

Under the Internal Revenue Code the donor has the right to change the ultimate remaindermen at any time before final distribution of the trust. So long as one charity is replaced with another IRS "qualified" charitable organization, the CRT's tax exempt status remains secure. Here's a tip: if you have a specific charity in mind (and you probably do), obtain their agreement to pay the creation costs of the CRT in return for your including in the trust declaration a waiver of your right to change remaindermen, making them the sure winners.

Calling the CRT a "qualified trust," is yet another name you will sometimes hear, meaning both that the CRT itself "qualifies" as tax exempt, and that the object of its ultimate distribution is also a "qualified" tax exempt organization.

That Congress should be so generous in allowing the grantor of a CRT so many tax breaks is perfectly consistent with the historic background we discussed - using taxes and tax concessions not just for revenue purposes, but to promote policy objectives as well. In exchange for his or her ultimate gift to charity, the CRT donor avoids many of the onerous asset-depleting tax burdens otherwise imposed by government - all in the name of promoting sweet charity which, it is rightly said, "begins at home."

With the CRT, it certainly does.

Let us now explore some of these attractive tax advantages that flow from the creation of a CRT.

Goodbye Capital Gains Tax:

It has become commonplace in America's quadrennial presidential election platforms for Republicans to call for reductions or repeal of the **capital gains tax** ("CGT") to stimulate investment and economic growth - while Democrats demand the tax be increased as a means of redistributing unjust gains from those who have much, to those who do not.

Lost in all the political rhetoric is the long-established availability of the charitable remainder trust, an effective bypass of the capital gains tax for a grantor who donates his or her appreciated property to the trust. The law is well-established that a transfer of appreciated property to a CRT is not a sale or exchange on which a capital gains tax is imposed.[4]

Hopefully, investments in real estate or other forms of property eventually mature, appreciating in value but too often declining in earnings or yield. Before this process proceeds too far, the prudent investor looks for new areas of investment with greater yields. But one very real roadblock gives pause before selling low-yield property and reinvesting elsewhere; the federal capital gains tax, which at this writing is set at the confiscatory maximum level of 28 percent.

Various states get into the act with their own CGT, for example, California, where it is now set at 11 percent. This produces a combined federal-state CGT of a whopping 36 percent - plus it pushes the taxpayer into a higher income tax bracket and raises his income taxes courtesy of that old devil "bracket creep."

To illustrate more vividly, suppose you are lucky enough to own a building worth $1 million currently, with a fully-depreciated acquisition basis of $40,000 - a prescient value judgment you made years ago - but now with a horrific taxable capital gain of $960,000. This means a combined federal and state CGT liability (if you live in California) of $344,832! That leaves $655,168 to reinvest, and if the first year pays a 10 percent return (again, lucky you), you get $65,517 in income - fully taxable at current federal and state income tax levels.

And don't forget **estate taxes**. If you are in the 50 percent estate tax bracket, and are unfortunate enough to die soon after your sale, your heirs will only get $327,584 after paying an estate tax of $327,584. Not much left of that $1 million building. How discouraging for those who remain alive.

But if you create a charitable remainder trust, then donate the building to the tax-exempt CRT, you pay **no capital gains tax** at all - zero, nor does the CRT trustee who sells the building later. The entire proceeds from the sale go into the trust for reinvestment - $1 million, tax free.[5] (The CRT assumes the donor's cost basis and the subsequent sale of the property by the trust results in a capital gain, but no tax is imposed - but see the related discussion of taxation of a beneficiary's CRT payout, below).

Remember that you will need a qualified appraisal of the value of real estate or any other property at the time of transfer to a CRT, and the trustee is required to report the transaction to the IRS. The transfer itself can be accomplished by a simple or quitclaim deed from the donor.

Of course low cost basis appreciated real property (either developed or undeveloped) is not the only candidate for donation to your CRT; it may be your closely-held family business that has skyrocketed in value over the years; it might be your personal residence that has done the same; or growth stocks or aggressive mutual funds that now would better be replaced with conservative, safe, high income investments.

A word about **mortgaged property** you might consider for donation to a CRT. Under IRS rules, if the property has been encumbered within five years prior to the proposed date of transfer to the trust, acceptance by the CRT, or any trust payment on the mortgage, would cause it to lose its tax-exempt status - and defeat the purpose of its creation. Or the transfer could receive tax treatment as a "bargain sale," making at least part of the appreciation immediately taxable to the donor as a capital gain. If the donor cannot pay off the mortgage before the transfer, there are possible ways to get

Of course such appreciated property gifts can obtain full current market value deductibility if donated to a qualified CRT, and in a sense while the money saved may not go to a family foundation, it will still be "all in the family."

Taxation of CRT Income Payouts:

This tax discussion raises an important point constantly to be kept in mind: cash distributions to beneficiaries of a CRT are taxable under a special three-tier income tax provision: first, as ordinary income to the beneficiary, if the trust has ordinary income; second, as a capital gain to the extent the trust has such a gain not taxed previously to the beneficiaries; and, third, as tax-free income, or a return of principal, if the distribution is in excess of ordinary income or capital gain.

Imposition of these beneficiary payout taxes suggests there may be an advantage to selling an appreciated asset first, then donating the cash proceeds to the CRT, thus assuring all future trust income will be tax free to the donor. When a CRT sells appreciated property, every subsequent annual distribution to beneficiaries in excess of ordinary income will be taxed as a capital gain, until the entire amount of the beneficiaries' original capital gain is paid. This means you may not escape some of the capital gains tax, but any payments are delayed and on the installment plan, and contingent on the type and amount of income the trust has.

The obvious solution is to fund the CRT with cash or non-appreciated assets allowing the trustee to invest in municipal bonds or securities that provide little or no current income, so there will be no immediate capital gains tax.

As you shall see in discussion that follows, there are several ways of structuring trust investments and income to minimize the beneficiary's income tax on annual payouts.

Charitable Remainder Trusts - Two Types:

The would-be donor contemplating the creation of a charitable remainder trust has two major types from which to choose, based on the technical form of payout desired in each case:

- **An annuity trust**, from which the donor receives a fixed annual dollar payout for a fixed number of years, or for a single lifetime or joint lifetimes (if married), for example, $80,000 a year, or a flat annual payment of eight percent of $1 million transferred to the trust. This annuity CRT more often is the choice of older persons wishing a dependable fixed income without being subjected to nerve-racking investment ups and downs.

- **A standard unitrust**, (as the most commonly used CRT is called), under which the donor receives for a similar period of time a fixed percentage of the trust assets, the exact dollar value of which must be determined annually, usually on the first of each year. For example, if the trust value increases from $1 million to $2 million, eight percent payments will double from $80,000 to $160,000.

Any good financial planner will usually recommend the unitrust because of the inflationary impact on an annuity trust. Even with current relatively low annual rates of inflation (as compared to the wild Jimmy Carter years in the 1970s with 18 percent inflation), the value of an annuity trust still declines rapidly. At four percent annual inflation, a fixed annuity will lose about one third of its real value in a ten-year period.

The IRS Says:

The Internal Revenue Code imposes strict requirements on a CRT, including:

- an irrevocable transfer of property to the trust, which must be reported by the donor and the trust on IRS forms;

- payment by the trust of a certain percentage of the value of the trust assets to one or more non-charitable beneficiaries for a period measured by their lifetimes, or up to a maximum of twenty years beyond their lifetimes;

- minimal payments of at least 5 percent of the value of the trust assets to the beneficiaries, a percentage that once chosen, cannot be changed during the life of the trust;[6]

- the remaining trust principal must be distributed to one or more qualified tax-exempt charitable institutions when the trust terminates - this being the key provision of a CRT.

Better Than A Pension Plan:

There is also a popular variation of the unitrust usually called an "**income only unitrust**," which can defer payment until a later date, thereby supplementing or substituting for a pension plan.[7] This type of CRT has become a very popular method of constructing a favorable tax retirement income fund.

As we have seen, the law requires distribution to beneficiaries of an amount equal to at least 5 percent of the trust assets each year, and in a typical unitrust the beneficiary must receive the annual payment, even if principal has to be invaded to make that payment. But this requirement can be waived if the trust declaration includes a direction that payments are to be made from trust "income only."

With careful planning and administration, the cash proceeds from the sale of original appreciated trust property can be reinvested in valuable assets producing little or no income in the early years of the trust operation, even as they increase in total value because of tax-free compounding.

Years later, when the beneficiary desires income for retirement, these low-yield trust assets can be sold, and funds shifted to high-yield investments paying the beneficiary the lesser of the fixed percentage of the value of trust assets, or from trust income which exceeds this percentage, for as long as he or she lives.

There can and should also be a **"make up" provision** in the trust declaration, requiring that whenever the specified percentage is not paid in any year because of the "income only" limitation forbidding invasion of principal, the cumulative deficit owed will be made up by increased payments in the subsequent years in which trust income does exceed the specified percentage of value.

Unlike 401K, Keogh, IRAs or other retirement plans, there is no limit to the amount one can contribute to a "net income" CRT, and some donor/beneficiaries continue to contribute on a monthly or other periodic basis until they need payback.

The Payout Rate - What and How?

Once you have chosen the unitrust route of tax breaks and increased income, two decisions have to be made - bearing in mind that under IRS rules these decisions, once made, are **irrevocable** for the life of the CRT:

- Recognizing that the IRS requires a minimum payout rate of 5 percent in order for a CRT to qualify, what payout rate do you want or need?

- How will you deal with the net income limitation?

Factors to Consider:

Here are some of the variables you should take into account before choosing the payout rate and the net income limitation; your age and that of your spouse, if you are married; the age of any other beneficiaries of the trust, assuming these may include your present or later born children; the fair market value of the appreciated asset you transfer to the CRT, and your tax basis in that asset; calculation of a reasonable rate of return on the re-invested proceeds after the assets are sold; the likely rate of inflation and the degree of anti-inflation protection you want built in by allowing tax-free compounding of value; the total amount of other assets and income you will have available other than the CRT payback.

Lastly, you should also determine the cost of future insurance premiums (or a one time premium), if you decide to create a **life insurance trust** for your heirs - about which we will have more to say in a moment.

A good CRT attorney and/or investment advisor should be able to draw a complete picture of the personal situation of each client based on information about the above factors, then provide an accurate dollar projection of how much your immediate charitable tax deduction will be, to what extent your annual income will increase each year, how much you will be able to leave your heirs, and what will be the eventual bequest you make to your chosen charities.

Choosing the Payout Rate:

Let's consider first the decision concerning establishing the payout rate itself.

If your immediate need is for high income levels, choosing a relatively high payout rate makes some sense. But if you are a donor beginning retirement, you should choose a payout rate that leaves sufficient funds in the CRT each year to keep your trust income ahead of projected inflation.

One approach would be to specify a relatively high payout rate, say 8 percent, and permit payment to be made from principal if trust net income is insufficient to meet this obligation to the beneficiary. In such a case investment would be almost entirely for growth purposes and well-capitalized growth stocks might be the place to look.

From 1946 through 1991, the best U.S. stocks have produced a return averaging about 12.7 percent annually. With an 8 percent payout and a growth stock investment policy, after administrative costs, it can reasonably be expected that about 4 percent of the fund could be added to trust principal each year.

The difficulty with this approach is that the annual rate of return left in the CRT each year must at least equal or surpass the annual rate of inflation, in order to preserve the purchasing power of future distributions and the ultimate remainder interest. An equal problem will be that annual payouts will be highly variable from year to year, because of inevitable fluctuations in the stock market. The donor/

beneficiary must be willing to put up with this variable payout prospect as the price of higher investment income.

Economic realities in the U.S. and the world will make it difficult, if not impossible, to produce a gross income return in excess of 8 percent, even if the CRT portfolio is invested totally in fixed income holdings, assuming the purchase of investment grade debt instruments. Expenses chargeable to income must also be subtracted, so the net income is likely to be even lower. For comparison's sake, consider that the highest quality long term bond yields have historically averaged about 4 to 5 percent a year. Assuming that the CRT will hold long term bonds to maturity, this part of the trust principal will not grow with inflation. Remember that if the CRT principal does not grow, neither does the income of the beneficiaries.

As an illustration of what happens when these factors are applied to CRT investment, a good case can be made that a conservative 5 percent payout rate will have the best all around results in the long term, _if_ there is the right mix of investments and careful management.

Assume in year one $1 million available for investment; a total trust investment mix of about 40 percent bonds with an annual 7 percent rate of return, 30 percent Standard and Poor's 500 stocks with a return of 12.7 percent, and another 30 percent split evenly between fast-growing U.S. and international small equities with rates of return of about 15 to 16 percent plus. Under this investment mix, with a 5 percent CRT payout rate, the $1 million will blossom in 20 years to about $4,800,000, of which $2,326,000 will be paid out to the beneficiaries.

Compare this with the choice of a higher 7 percent CRT payout rate; the same $1 million invested totally in safe no-growth long term bonds at 7 percent net annual return, in 20 years will leave only $1 million in principal, after cumulative annual beneficiary payments of $1.4 million.

Check that comparative 20-year record again: a 5 percent payout rate with a carefully mixed investment policy produces $2.3 million in benefits; a 7 percent payout rate with a no growth investment policy produces $1.4 million in benefits. The 5 percent choice ends up with $4.8 million remainder for charity, the 7 percent, only $1 million - each with concomitant charitable income tax deductions for the donor in the first year based on the rate of payout chosen in year one.

The Net Income Limitation:

The second major initial decision for the donor is how to deal with the net income limitation on the CRT payout.

The decision here will largely depend on your CRT investment policy, how immediate your need for income may be, or whether you wish to postpone income until a later time. There are four possibilities:

(1) Require annual payout whether or not there is net income sufficient to pay it, i.e. take some out of principal. But keep in mind what happens then. The effect of failing to meet a required payout by even a small percentage over many years has some dramatic results. Assuming $1 million invested, an 8 percent payout and a 7 percent overall investment return, the principal would shrink to $739,700 in 30 years.

(2) Limit annual payout to available net income, but include a "catch up" provision allowing shortfalls to be paid later out of future year excess income. This is convenient for younger donors who don't want much income early in the life of the trust, later switching to high income growth stocks when they retire. This "growth without income" strategy early on can be accomplished by investing in growth securities, zero coupon bonds and deferred annuities. In effect, this is using an appreciated asset to fund a pension plan substitute, without all the reporting and restrictions imposed on pension plans.

(3) Limit annual payout to the lowest of either the established annual payout amount or, the available net income. If the CRT is funded with non-liquid assets like closely held corporation stock or real estate with little current income, this option is the best.

(4) Impose no net income limitations, thereby leaving open the possibility of employing a more growth oriented investment approach to produce an increased total return. This makes sense when the CRT is funded with liquid assets which can easily be invested and re-invested - and when there is full-time, careful management.

These sorts of multi-year dollar projections are easily done by computer and should be available before choosing the rate of return and any net income limitations. Also note that when we use the phrase "annual payout" in all of these alternatives, that includes the possibility you may elect to have payments semi-annually or quarterly, both of which are common.

The "bottom line" as they say, on these choices is that while a CRT is a very useful investment device, in order to be successful the donor has to take a hard-eyed look at future economic realities, including inflation and long-term rates of return, before choosing an approach that matches the donor's goals. It also means consideration of a lower payout rate, which may easily be more productive in the long haul.

On a related point, trust donors can establish a longer term CRT that benefits them during their lives, then afterwards benefits successor generations of children and grandchildren. This has the effect of maximizing the cumulative impact of tax-free compounding of value. Careful planning must go into such an arrangement in order to avoid adverse estate tax and generation-skipping transfer taxes, but it can be done - and the many years of compounding makes it all worthwhile.

Investing Trust Assets In A Commercial Annuity

The trustee could immediate sell the appreciated assets transferred to the trust and invest the proceeds in a commercial annuity. The investment strategy would be to grow the annuity fund as much as possible during the pre-retirement years. To accomplish this, the trustee would choose a deferred annuity.

Because the trust is not a "natural person," annual increases in the value of the annuity would be treated as constructive receipt of income by the trust. The trust agreement would have to define income for trust accounting and distribution purposes so as to include only income actually received by the trust. As a result, there would be no trust income and no need to make distributions during the pre-retirement years.

However, if an income were needed or panted prior to retirement, the trustee could simply withdraw amounts from the annuity and, assuming the fund had grown in value, the full amount of the withdrawal would be trust income and could be immediately distributed -- up to the income value limit of the trust in that year plus any accumulated deficits.

After retirement, the trustee could withdraw a reasonable amount each year to provide a lifetime retirement income.

The Role of the Trustee:

As you can readily understand from the discussion of charitable remainder trust investment policy, the role of the trustee is crucial to success. While trust management can be complex and time consuming, in most situations the trustee can usually handle the work with occasional assistance from an attorney or investment planner.

There is a natural tendency on the part of a donor to want to serve as the CRT trustee, and the law does not forbid this dual role. However, as noted before, this arrangement immediately raises questions of conflict of interest, especially about the character of investments the trustee may choose. A donor who does not serve as trustee still has a significant degree of continuing control, because the donor can reserve the right in the trust declaration to change the trustee at any time. The donor can also ask the trustee to change the nature of the CRT investments from low-yield growth assets to high income investments, at any time the donor/beneficiary needs steady income.

Realistically, the creation and operation of a CRT usually means there is a close working relationship between the donor/beneficiary and their personally chosen trustee. In a serious dispute, the beneficiary can always look to the courts to protect his or her interests, if the trustee is thought to be engaged in activity inimicable to the best interests of the trust.

The **duties of a trustee** include selling at the best price possible the appreciated assets transferred to the trust; investing the proceeds from the sale in the manner that will best advance the trust goals; arranging the cash flow needed for periodic distributions to beneficiaries; annual evaluation of trust assets; filing federal trust tax forms (IRS forms 1041A and 5227); maintaining a trust bank account and accurate records of income, expenses, payouts and accumulations of income and capital gains; and, informing beneficiaries of how they must personally report annual payouts for tax purposes.

For obvious reasons, if the donor/beneficiary does serve as a trustee, it is highly advisable to have a co-trustee with full authority to make the annual value determination required in a unitrust CRT, so there will be no question about impartiality.

Another approach that is little known, but of great utility, is for the donor to be the trustee, but use a firm specializing in the administration of charitable remainder trusts to handle the accounting, tax returns, and often, retaining investment managers.

The "Prudent Investor" Rule:

Keep in mind that the trustee must act in a fiduciary capacity on behalf of the interests of both parties to the CRT - the donor/beneficiary and the remainderman. This means an impartial administration of trust assets to provide both favorable current income, and also preservation of the largest possible remaining corpus for the designated charity.

The Third Restatement of the Law of Trusts, section 227, the authoritative treatise on such matters, imposes a duty on a trustee to manage a trust as a "prudent investor," balancing the rights of the beneficiary and the remainderman in light of the terms of the trust declaration, payout requirements and all other circumstances including inflationary considerations.

The difficulty arises when market conditions make it impossible to satisfy both parties' best interests. Then the trustee is expected to look for direction to the donor's intent as expressed in the trust declaration - yet another reason the drafting of that basic document is of such great importance. The question then becomes, did the grantor intend to favor the remainderman over the current income beneficiary? Under the codified Third Restatement rules, a trustee would rarely implement an investment policy that clearly favors one side over the other, unless the trust declaration unambiguously directed such a course. This is so because the Restatement suggests that a trustee can be held personally financially responsible for investing in a manner that favors the beneficiary at the expense of the remainderman, especially if the diminished principal loses purchasing power due to inflation.

For example, a trust arrangement which allows the beneficiary to receive payment out of principal when current income is insufficient, clearly harms the interest of the remainderman - an inherent conflict of interest for the trustee. This dilemma can be avoided so long as the overall rate of return (current income plus capital appreciation) meets the payout requirement, and thus keeps the corpus intact. But when the trustee must figure in inflation, principal may have to be invaded to pay the beneficiary. As we have already discussed, setting the payout rate at the minimum 5 percent will usually avoid this conflict, but higher payout rates might guarantee the problem.

The practical solution is to set the payout rate as low as possible (5 percent), so that an experienced trustee's wisely diversified portfolio of investments can earn interest and dividends sufficient to meet all current income needs with inflation taken into account.

Don't forget in this discussion of "competing interests" between CRT beneficiaries and the remainderman; the sole policy reason the law allows and encourages charitable remainder trusts (and the concomitant benefits to donors), is the ultimate objective of promoting charitable organizations and the achievement of their goals by tax-exempt private financing. The IRS does not look favorably on operating a sham CRT providing bountiful lifetime rewards to its donor/ beneficiary, while ultimately short changing the charitable organization it was created to help. Follow that route and it leads to enormous retroactive tax liabilities, including interest and penalties stretching back over the years to the CRT's date of creation.

In the midst of all these shifting variables, the "prudent investor" trustee can easily get caught "in the middle." These problems should suggest how important it is to choose a qualified CRT trustee who, in fact, has your complete trust.

Taking Care of the Children:

There are solid practical reasons why a CRT should have as its beneficiaries a husband and wife, and not their children. These reasons are taxes.

If the sole individual CRT beneficiary is the donor, federal law exempts the entire value of the property donated to the CRT from all **federal gift and estate taxes**. This tax avoidance is a considerable advantage, at a time when both these federal taxes are assessed at from 37 percent to 60 percent of the total value of the estate property. If the donor's spouse is also a beneficiary, the value of that interest is reportable as a taxable gift, but it fully qualifies for a marital gift tax deduction.

If the couples' children (or others) are also named as beneficiaries, their interests are taxable gifts to the extent their interests exceed the allowable annual exclusions. Annual gifts of cash or other property worth $10,000 or less, often called "annual exclusion gifts," may be made by a donor free of any federal gift or estate tax. In order to qualify for this exclusion the gift must be of a "present interest" in the property. Trust gifts do not usually qualify unless the trust is specially designed to accommodate such "present interest" gifts.

In addition to federal estate and gift taxes, any grandchildren's CRT interest would also be subject to the federal "generation skipping" tax of a flat 55 percent in excess of $1 million in gifts made to them during the donor's lifetime. One bright spot is that property given to a qualified charity is fully deductible against any gift or estate taxes.

If one does not include their children as beneficiaries of the CRT, how does one "make it up" to the kids for their "lost" value of the $1 million building that ultimately becomes a gift to the charitable remainderman?

There are several ways to accomplish this worthy parental goal, but first let's consider some simple tax arithmetic to lay a basis for a suggested solution.

When a building (or anything else) valued at $1 million is donated to a CRT, it is received tax free. As we have seen, with a capital gains tax the $1 million would have been reduced to $731,200 in after tax cash. But $1 million invested by the CRT at an expected 8 percent return gives the donor $80,000 annually in income, rather than $58,496, the annual amount of cash after the capital gains tax. That means a net bonanza of $21,504 each year. And here's where the solution to the children's inheritance problem is achieved.

Using $15,000 of the net bonanza money, the parents can fund an **irrevocable life insurance trust,** (also called a "wealth replacement" or inheritance trust), with their children as named beneficiaries.

Many couples chose to have their life insurance trust purchase a "last to die" or "survivorship" policy covering them jointly. Such a policy is much cheaper and is not payable, as indicated, until the last of the two parents dies. Donating a portion of their increased income from their CRT to their life insurance trust, about $15,000 annually, for ten years will allow purchase of a "last to die" whole life policy paying about $750,000. This inheritance is far more than the net value that $1 million building would have produced had it not gone to the CRT, but remained a part of the parents' estate to be ravaged by federal taxes.

The $750,000 insurance payout figure is approximate because, as in all insurance policies, the exact premiums and payout depends on variables concerning the person or persons insured. This figure is a quote from an insurance company based on a non-smoking 65 year-old couple in good health at the time the life insurance is purchased. Some insurance companies will include an optional clause guaranteeing that if both insured parents die within four years of each other, the company will pay out 222 percent of the face value of the policy. At least one spouse must be under age 70 and in good health to obtain this lucrative policy rider, but that means double the money for your heirs.

Even if the IRS somehow successfully attacked this sum as being taxable as part of the parents' estate, and even if the estate was in the 55 percent tax bracket, that means on a $1 million policy paying $2.22 million, after tax proceeds would still equal the $1 million. It's worth the gamble and probably more likely than winning the state lottery.

Using the life insurance trust route, everybody should be pleased; the parents have added net lifetime income from the CRT, the children have an equal or greater inheritance, and the charity of your choice benefits greatly in the end.

A word of caution. Before establishing a life insurance trust and having it purchase any life insurance policies, all the personal health variables, actual premium costs and payouts should be realistically assessed and quotations obtained in writing from the prospective insurer. This is not an area to be left to hopeful promises from an eager insurance salesperson. A firm administering charitable remainder trusts can usually get the best deals on wealth replacement life insurance, as they are experienced in working with insurance companies who understand the purpose of the policy, and in obtaining competitive quotations.

After all, your children deserve the best - guaranteed money.

Internationalizing Your CRT

The CRT can be a foreign trust, but it is not permitted to be a "grantor trust." Any non-U.S. trust created by a U.S. person which has a U.S. beneficiary is automatically a "grantor turst." But, for CRT purposes only, the status of the donor/grantor and his spouse are ignored.

The CRT can be a foreign trust yet not be a grantor trust if the only U.S. beneficiary of the trust is either the grantor or his spouse. But a non-U.S. corporation can be the beneficiary, and this is the solution recommended by most international tax planners. An international, albeit foreign charity, might be named as the recipient of the remainder interest. The prospective charity would be located in a U.S. possession, which is not deemed to be a part of the United States (see Code Section 7701(a)(9), but does qualify under Section 170(c) to receive the remainder interest. The charity does not need to be named. The CRT need only provide that the charity must be a non-U.S. entity which nonetheless qualifies under Code Section 170(c).

This brief summary of internationalizing a CRT only begins to touch on the complexities of the subject, but in combination with other entities, including the hybrid company, the international CRT can be an excellent way of removing appreciated asset values from the U.S.

Because the subject is one that is highly specialized, it is best to work with a firm of experts already experienced in creating these international structures. My recommendation is:

> Skye Fiduciary Services Limited
> Attn: New Clients Information
> 2 Water Street
> Ramsey, Isle of Man 1M8 1JP
> United Kingdom
> Telephone: (44-1) 624- 816117
> Fax: (44-1) 624- 816645; attn: New Clients Information

(As many of my readers will know, the Isle of Man is a very useful tax haven separate from Great Britain, but since most of the world's post offices won't know where it is, it is easier to humor them by including Great Britain in the address.)

Skye Fiduciary Services Limited are specialist consultants, designers of offshore and international fiduciary structures, and you will find my recommendation repeated in the hybrid companies chapter.

The chairman of the firm is Charles Cain, who was managing director of the second merchant bank to open on the Isle of Man, before he started his own business. He and his associates operate what I have no hesitation in calling the oldest and most experienced offshore corporate and trust management business in the Isle of Man.

They can provide a full range of company management and trust management services. But it is their services in designing company and trust services that make them unique, and they can combine entities from several jurisdictions to create the most viable structure for the client. These can include trading companies, offshore family and charitable foundations, asset protection arrangements, and secure yet anonymous holding vehicles.

They also have the necessary expertise to ensure that offshore structures for U.S. persons precisely fit the required characterization under the Internal Revenue Code (and can develop tax efficient structures for those intending to immigrate to the U.S.).

In Summary:

Because the tax code is constantly being changed by Congress, there is never any assurance the multiple benefits of charitable remainder trusts will always be available in its present form. With so many donors, beneficiaries and charitable organizations all giving and receiving many hundreds of millions of dollars every year under this system, it is unlikely such a popular and long standing feature of tax law will be changed substantially. But like the recent limitation imposed on gifts of appreciated property to family foundations, the CRT also can be modified to curb its benefits.

The moral of the story - the time is now for you to investigate and decide whether the charitable remainder trust is the right way for you, your family and your favorite charity.

USING A FAMILY PARTNERSHIP TO LOWER TAXES

One of the most versatile and powerful tools in the ongoing struggle to save taxes and protect your wealth from frivolous or vengeful lawsuits -- not to mention absurd liability claims -- is the family limited partnership (FLP). One common use of FLPs is to reduce your income tax liability. As an estate planning vehicle, FLPs can also help you avoid inheritance taxes.

As an asset protection vehicle, FLPs combine the best of both worlds; they allow you to keep 100% control of your assets while at the same time placing them beyond the reach of creditors. Although usually used by Americans, for foreign investors with U.S. assets or business, a U.S. limited partnership might be the first line of defense against exposure to the lawsuit-happy legal environment in the U.S. Even if a creditor wins a judgment against you, he may not be able to collect a dime from your partnership interest -- a fact that is inclined to make even the most pugnacious adversaries eager to settle.

We'll outline how to use a FLP to achieve each of these advantages in due course. But first, let's establish exactly what we mean by a family limited partnership. A partnership is merely an association of two or more persons (or other legal entities, such as corporations or trusts) in some kind of joint venture.

According to Section 761 of the U.S. Internal Revenue Code, a partnership is "a syndicate, group, pool, joint venture, business, or other unincorporated organization through or by means of which any business, financial operation, or venture is carried on..." In a limited partnership, there are two kinds of participants -- general partners and limited partners.

The general partners have management and control of the partnership's assets and activities. And they are liable for any debts or claims against the partnership. Limited partners generally have no say in the running of the partnership's affairs, and they have absolutely no personal liability.

A typical FLP might have a husband and wife with a general partnership interest of perhaps 10% and children (and perhaps relatives) with limited partnership interests totaling

90%. Such an FLP might contain the family business, or other assets. Note that in this example, the husband and wife, as general partners, maintain 100% control of the FLP, despite owning only 10% of it.

Income and estate tax benefits

For tax purposes, income earned by a FLP is reportable on the individual income tax returns of the partners. (Usually income is allocated among partners according to the fraction of their partnership interest.) This means that you can use the FLP to spread the tax liability for family business among family members -- such as minor children -- who will be in a lower tax bracket.

FLPs can also be used as a simple means of giving the family assets to children in small amounts in order to avoid inheritance taxes. In this case, the FLP would initially be set up with the husband and wife having both a general partnership interest of 10% and a limited partnership interest of 90%.

Each year these parents could give a fraction of their limited partnership interest to their children (and heirs). Each parent can give $10,000 of their limited partnership interest to each child every year without incurring any U.S. gift tax liability.

In this way, the parents' taxable estate can be substantially reduced over a period of years. What's more, even though they may have given away 90% interest to their children, as general partners, they enjoy complete control of all FLP assets.

Asset protection

Suppose you are sued, and a creditor wins a judgment against you. Suppose further that you have your home and other major assets in a FLP. In general, a limited partnership may not be dissolved simply because one partner is sued. In most jurisdictions, a creditor cannot touch any of the partnership assets. At best, he can hope to obtain something known as a "charging order" against your partnership interest. This will entitle him only to any distributions you would receive as a general or a limited partner.

However, you remain the general partner despite the judgment. This means that *when and if any distributions are ever paid out to partners remains entirely under your control.* As you can imagine, a creditor armed with a charging order, waiting for you to declare a distribution, may have to wait a very long time indeed.

Furthermore, the fact that you have a creditor looking over your shoulder doesn't mean you can't continue to enjoy the benefits of the FLP. For example, general partners often receive a salary for their services to the partnership. You can also receive advances or loans from the FLP.

You just can't receive any benefit that might be classified as a distribution. For this reason, having your assets in an FLP may make you a much less likely target for a lawsuit in the first place.

One word of caution: What we have discussed so far is the asset protection afforded by a FLP to someone who is sued as an individual. If he has his assets in an FLP, he will enjoy the benefits we have described. However, it is important to keep in mind that you as an individual are not the only potential victim of a lawsuit. Your FLP itself could also be sued.

For example, suppose the family business is organized as a limited partnership and the business is sued for malpractice or breach of contract. If the FLP itself loses in court, then the charging order concept does not apply -- and all of its assets are available to creditors for attachment.

For this reason, it is often wise to divide assets with liability exposure among several partnerships or corporations. For example, many taxi companies establish a separate corporation for every single vehicle. That way, a judgment against one part of the business need not necessarily imperil all the others.

Accordingly, the most effective asset protection scheme will almost always make use of several of the structures available -- such as corporations, foreign corporations, and foreign trusts. It is indeed possible to make your financial defenses truly impregnable.

Remember, too, as you read the following sections, that your investments can be further protected by various combinations of family limited partnerships and trusts, depending upon your individual needs. Not every investment needs to be placed in your personal name -- and since the FLP is tax neutral, or even offers tax savings, it may be an ideal vehicle for making some of these investments.

Asset protection and tax savings

While it is very nice to save on estate taxes, most would be much more interested in saving taxes this year, right now while you are still alive. The "estate plan", when properly implemented has the delightful side effect of making excellent use of your children before they thought they could, or were inclined to be, helpful. Remember that children over the age of 14 have their very own tax brackets which start at 0% and linger at 15% for a time or so, just as yours did, and only after more income than they will make or than you need to give them for their support jump up to the higher tax brackets. It is possible, especially for the self-employed,to cut the total tax bite in half by simply spreading the tax liability among family members.

At this point you say, "Now just a minute, I know what you are about to say, and I assure you that giving assets or income to my children at this stage of their teenage lives is a type of suicide that I do not contemplate." You are right! Let me assure you that no one is foolish enough to suggest that any assets or income should be put under the "control" of children, who at the age of 16 think that a 944 Porsche turbo something or other is an appropriate investment.

The Family Limited Partnerships, and Children's Trusts allow income to be attributed to the children's tax brackets while leaving the "control" and "use" to more responsible parties. In the case of the Family Limited Partnership, the more responsible party would be you. In the case of the Children's Trust, that person would be a trusted other. However, the children and their guardians, and once again, you, would be able to have lower tax bracketed dollars available for luxuries such as family trips, piano lessons, math camp, private schools, college, medical school, etc.

Consider this: Mr. and Mrs. Business Partners set up a Children's Trust for their children and funded it with real estate in which their business was housed. The kids wanted the building to be a retail space suitable for an ice cream parlor, but since they were not in charge of the decisions, the building purchased was an 80,000 square foot steel and block industrial building suitable for the parent's manufacturing business.

The business, which had a good profit picture and cash flow, paid rent to the Children's Trust, thereby writing off the lease payments at a higher tax bracket than the children's tax bracket and accepting the payments in the lower children's bracket. Tax savings were realized each year. In addition, Mr. and Mrs. Business Partners suggest to the Children's Trust, that, with the profits from the lease, it could buy office equipment which it could lease to the business on a "one year renewable lease" for market lease payments, i.e., 75% of the value of the equipment **each year.** More tax savings were realized.

It is only incidental to this discussion on the advantages of the "estate plan" to mention that when Mr. and Mrs. Business Partners went out of business because the widgets which the parents were manufacturing were replaced by a new super duper better thing, the Children's Trust survived the parent's bankruptcy and with the appreciated value of the real estate and value of the still owned equipment, sold its assets and loaned Mr. and Mrs. Business Partners $500,000.00 to start a new business.

The above examples are illustrative of the old adage, "divide and conquer." If they only file a joint return, no married couple will ever get ahead tax wise. If through a proper estate plan additional entities are created the serve the dual purpose of providing lawsuit and asset protection while dividing income into lower tax brackets. Creating additional entities does itself provide a record keeping and filing burden. It is bad enough facing April 15th each year with one incomprehensible form! However, if you are unwilling to pay attention to the details there are others who will do it for a fee. Failure to care may result in exposure to judgments and the possible greater burden of "starting over."

One major caution must be mentioned, as some of these asset protection techniques are taking on aspects of a fad. The courts can set aside a transaction on the basis that it is a sham, despite what your fancy paperwork says. A family limited partnership formed on the eve of a judgment, with no business purpose and no purpose other than evading the creditor, is likely to be set aside by the court. The same is true of trust arrangements made in the same way.

These problems can be avoided by making such arrangements in advance, having sound and proper purposes other than avoiding ones just debts, and to some extent using foreign jurisdictions to make seizure more difficult.

It is important to stress that there are no "magic bullets" in asset protection, and there is no instant solution. Setting up an asset protection plan -- whether it be partnerships, offshore trusts, domestic trusts, or some combination, requires expert advice.

YOUR OWN HIGH-YIELDING, SUPER-SAFE, TAX-FREE OFFSHORE ACCOUNT -- AND NOT EVEN THE IRS HAS TO KNOW

Most people think of annuities as simply investment vehicles. When the topic becomes Swiss annuities, however, these investments take on an added dimension of safety. What most people don't realize is that Swiss annuities, along with their competitive rates, steady dividends, and security, offer another important benefit -- that of asset protection.

In recent years a great many people, including professionals, directors of companies, and investors (both large and small), have become increasingly concerned about protecting their assets from liability claims and creditors. In the past, those concerned with protecting their wealth would often set up trusts. Indeed, in response to this growing need, several offshore companies have begun offering trusts that are designed specifically to protect one's assets from creditors.

Largely lost amid the hype and various types of investments being offered are Swiss annuities.

Swiss annuities are products of the Swiss insurance industry. This alone sets them apart from other investment options, because the integrity of the Swiss insurance industry is protected by Swiss law. Insurance products, including annuities, enjoy that protection in a rather unique, but extremely solid manner.

In general legal proceedings, creditors are permitted to seize insurance policies, bought by debtors, to pay off money owed during a collection procedure against the debtor. Creditors may also have insurance policies included in a debtor's estate in a bankruptcy proceeding. This type of legal proceeding is also usually true of Swiss law (according to Article 79, Paragraph 1 of the Swiss Insurance Act), provided that the policy owner has designated a third part as the beneficiary of the policy. The designation of the beneficiary is voided if the insured individual declares bankruptcy or if his or her creditors seize the policy.

However, if the policy owner of the Swiss insurance policy, or annuity, has *irrevocably* designated a third party as his or her beneficiary, or if the owner of the policy has *irrevocably or revocably* designated his or her spouse and/or descendants as beneficiaries of the policy, the policy is protected from the policy owner's creditors (Article 80, Swiss Insurance Act).

At first glance when considering using a Swiss annuity or insurance policy for asset protection, one might think that the policy owner must relinquish control over his or her assets to protect them. However, at closer inspection, it becomes clear that this is an excellent method for securing protection. By revocably designating a spouse and/or descendants as beneficiaries, the assets are protected from creditors. The key word of course is *revocable*. The owner not only gains protection, but he or she retains control of the annuity. As time goes by, and the conditions and demands of life change, the owner of the policy may review his or her financial situation and decide to revoke the designation of beneficiaries. Obviously, depending on circumstances, policy owners may simply leave the designated beneficiaries as they are, may decide to buy more annuities, or extend the terms of existing ones. Unquestionably, the policy owner enjoys a large measure of flexibility with asset management.

Swiss Annuities and Asset Protection

One of the most vital areas of the Swiss financial markets is the insurance industry. While Swiss banks are associated with safety and conservative management, the insurance industry has not had a single company failure in more than 130 years. This is a record that surpasses even the steadiness of Swiss banks.

About twenty insurance companies compete in Switzerland. All are financially sound and managed with an eye for safety and high return. Usually, the two conditions -- safety and high yield regarding investments -- are mutually exclusive. High yield implies risk. Unlike the insurance industries in other countries, however, insurance companies in Switzerland enjoy unique tax advantages. Coupled with efficient and intelligent management, Swiss insurance companies are able to offer a variety of steady and productive investment opportunities.

Of all the investment options offered by Swiss insurance companies, annuities provide excellent benefits and can be used for asset protection. The typical annuity is an investment that enables the investor to place money in a tax-advantaged plan. A common purpose of many annuities is to set aside money for retirement. A major benefit of annuities is that they allow investors to defer taxes on savings. Thus, the investor is able to build assets more quickly than can be done with other, often more risky, investments. Annuities can be used to save money for a variety of purposes, however, they are most frequently used as retirement accounts. For the individual concerned with asset protection, annuities provide a means of achieving solid returns while deferring taxes.

Annuities, especially Swiss annuities with the added features of their strength and potential for asset protection, possess many prominent advantages:

- Annuities can be structured so that there is no investment ceiling. The annuity owner can contribute as much as he or she wants each year.

- Because annuities provide tax-deferment, the money in the account grows faster than other investments with similar rates of return. Furthermore, many investors wait to take money out of annuities after they have retired and are in a lower tax bracket. In this way they pay less taxes and save more of their money.

- Annuities offer superior security for the investor's family. Should the investor die before the earnings of the annuity are distributed, beneficiaries can receive the full value of the annuity.

- Record-keeping for annuities is simple. Because taxes are deferred, it is not necessary to file forms regarding annuities with the IRS until payments begin.

- Asset protection via Swiss annuities is much cheaper than asset protection through many other investments, particularly trusts. Establishing a trust, and then paying   for management of it, can require rather hefty fees. Any fees through Swiss annuities are minor, and asset protection carries no extra cost at all. It is a standard feature of any Swiss annuity or insurance policy.

- Annuities are flexible investment options. Beneficiaries, for example, may be changed depending upon changing personal situations. In the case of divorce the annuity owner may wish to remove his or her former spouse from the annuity as beneficiary.

The Many Added Advantages of Swiss Annuities

Swiss annuities offer many advantages over annuities offered in other countries. Annuities have, in fact, been offered since the early 1970s, however, the financial markets have seen truly impressive growth in the area of annuities during the last few years. In the United States alone, the sales of annuities run close to $50 billion every year.

Despite their growing popularity, many people remain confused about annuities. Some think of them as being much the same as a mutual fund. While annuities can offer similar rates of returns, they have a major advantage -- annuities defer taxes until retirement. Mutual funds do not. Further, annuities can be set up in a way that once the investor begins to draw on the funds, he or she will receive regular payments for life.

The costs for annuities are also different than the costs for mutual funds. Because annuities are offered by insurance companies, for most annuities, the investor does not have to pay any commissions or front-end load fees. In most cases, there are penalties for withdrawing funds early, but these usually apply only for the first few years after an annuity has been opened. Swiss annuities, however, limit any "surrender" fees to the first year. This is a major consideration and advantage for investors in purchasing Swiss annuities over the annuities sold elsewhere.

Swiss annuities offer even more benefits. In many countries where annuities are offered, including the U.S., annuities are loosely regulated in comparison to other types of investments. In Switzerland, annuities are closely regulated, reducing risks to investors. Unlike the annuities sold in the U.S., which are backed by the dollar, which has been eroding steadily in value and purchasing power throughout the last hundred years, Swiss annuities are backed by the Swiss franc. The Swiss franc is far more stable, because it is backed by gold.

The payout plan for Swiss annuities is flexible and the payout is guaranteed. Indeed, payments can be set up to meet the individual needs of each investor. Payments can be sent out on annual, semi-annual, or quarterly schedules (a monthly schedule is available to Swiss residents). Although payments are denominated in Swiss francs, investors may instruct the insurance company to convert the payment into any currency they wish. Of course, they may make the conversions themselves at their bank in Switzerland. The Swiss insurance company will gladly send the payment to the investor, wherever he or she lives, or to the investor's bank.

In regards to taxes, Swiss annuities are also very attractive investments. Swiss annuities are exempt from the 35% withholding tax that foreigners who hold Swiss bank accounts must pay on their interest. Perhaps more importantly, investors do not have to report Swiss annuities to either Swiss or U.S. tax agencies, although U.S. buyers of Swiss annuities must pay a 1% federal excise tax on the purchase of the policy. IRS Form 720 requires only that a calculation for an excise tax of 1% be made for the purchase of any foreign policy, however, no details of the policy need be reported. The excise tax payment is required to be paid only once at the time of the purchase of the policy. It is the investor's responsibility to report it. Swiss insurance companies do not provide any information regarding the purchase of annuities, the amount or number of payments made into the policy, or any earnings to government agencies in the U.S. or Switzerland. Confidentiality is assured.

Along with all this, Swiss annuities provide asset protection at no additional cost. In many cases, policies can be designed to afford protection from the beneficiary's creditors as well as the creditors of the annuity owner. If the annuity is structured so that payments are provided for the beneficiary, but the beneficiary has not made any contributions to the purchase of the annuity, any proceeds of the annuity are protected from the beneficiary's creditors. The annuity owner may thus protect the annuity from his creditors and also any creditors of his beneficiary. This can be particularly useful if the beneficiary is subject to the same potential claims as the annuity owner.

The only way that creditors can seize an annuity is if they can prove that the designation of beneficiaries was an attempt to defraud the creditors, as noted in the Swiss debt collection bankruptcy act. Fraud, however, is very difficult to prove. One scenario would be if the annuity and designation of the beneficiaries was made within six months of the date the annuity owner filed for bankruptcy. Another would be if it could be proven that the designation of beneficiaries was made with the intent to shield assets because the investor knew that he or she was about to declare bankruptcy. In this case, if the designation of beneficiaries was made within five years before the owner of the annuity declared bankruptcy or has his assets seized, creditors may be able to seize the annuity. Intent to defraud, though, would have to be proved.

Attempting to prove that an investor did in fact plan to defraud creditors could be established only under strict and specific circumstances. Most importantly, it would have to be shown that the annuity owner was in financial desperation -- meaning that he was already carrying an overload of debt -- and that he made the designation of beneficiaries in response to that indebtedness. On the other hand, fraud could not be proven if, at the time he or she bought the annuity and designated a beneficiary, the annuity owner had enough assets to cover his or her debts. Moreover, showing that he or she could not foresee the coming indebtedness would make it almost impossible for a creditor to prove fraud.

Swiss annuities are strongly protected from creditors. This includes the American IRS. If annuities are structured properly, and no intent to defraud can be proven, the annuities are virtually untouchable. Investors may be assured that their assets in the annuity are protected and that the proceeds of the annuity will remain intact.

Much of this protection arises from the fact that Swiss annuities are protected by Swiss law. For example, for a creditor to move ahead with a collection procedure against a foreign debtor's Swiss annuities, the creditor may seek to seize the assets of the debtor's annuity in Switzerland. If the creditor attempts to seize assets of the debtor in the debtor's home country, the creditor may file for the recognition of the foreign bankruptcy decree in Switzerland.

Nevertheless, no matter how the creditor may attempt to seize the assets of the annuity owner, the creditor's actions will be subject to Swiss law. The rules that oversee the protection of insurance policies will be in full effect. Since the investor owns a Swiss annuity, Swiss law now takes precedence over the laws that may govern collection efforts in his or her home country. It does not matter where the investor's home country is, or where he or she currently lives. If the investor owns a Swiss annuity, the rights included with the contract are considered to be in Switzerland. In effect, the investor's Swiss assets enjoy an excellent degree of protection.

The only way creditors may seize a Swiss annuity is to prove that the investor bought the annuity and designated beneficiaries with the intent to defraud his or her creditors. And that is a difficult case to prove.

Even if creditors institute proceedings in the home country of the investor, for example the United States, and a judgment is passed, the judgment will not be recognized by Swiss law. No payments would be made by the Swiss insurance company to the creditor.

A Brief Summary of the Benefits of Swiss Annuities

Swiss annuities offer numerous benefits to investors. Although annuities can be purchased in many countries around the world, none can match the overall advantages Swiss annuities provide. Here are the major benefits:

- *Asset protection*. By irrevocably designating a third party as the beneficiary, or by revocably or irrevocably designating a spouse and/or descendants as beneficiaries, the policy owner is able to protect the policy from creditors. Provided that the annuityprovides for payments to the beneficiary, and that beneficiary has not made any contribution to the purchase of the annuity, the annuity is also protected from potential creditors of the beneficiary. It should be noted that the asset protection is guaranteed by Swiss law and does not cost the investor anything. It comes with

Swiss annuities. Virtually the only way a creditor can seize an annuity is to prove that the investor purchased the annuity with the intent to defraud the creditor. This is most difficult to prove in Swiss courts. Even if a judgment is rendered in another country, that judgment has no standing in Swiss courts. The Swiss have a strong reputation for protecting the assets of their investors.

- ***Financial safety.*** Any investment sold in Switzerland is backed by the country's financial strength. Switzerland is considered by many authorities to be the financially strongest country in the world. Unlike the currencies of many other countries, including the United States, the Swiss franc is backed by gold. The Swiss insurance industry has not suffered a failure in over a century.

- ***Swiss annuities offer excellent rates and dividends.*** Because of Switzerland's advantageous tax rates and generally sound financial practices, Swiss annuities offer rates and dividends that are extremely competitive with annuities offered elsewhere.

- ***Tax savings.*** Swiss annuities, tied to the Swiss franc, are free from Swiss taxes. American investors enjoy additional tax advantages. Earnings on annuities are not taxed during a tax-deferred period. Moreover, they are not taxable until income is paid or the annuity is liquidated. Since many investors choose to take income from annuities after they have retired, the income is generally taxed at a lower rate.

- **Savings on fees.** Whereas many investments, trusts for example, have high fees and administration costs, Swiss annuities have no front-end or back-end load fees. Further, unlike annuities in other countries, the investor in Swiss annuities may cancel at any time with no loss of principal. Only if the annuity is canceled during the first year is a small penalty fee due. However, after the first year, all principal and interest and dividends are returned to the investor with no penalty. For many annuities around the world, cancellation times may extend up to five years.

- **Swiss privacy regarding finances.** Swiss annuities enjoy the famous Swiss privacy tradition. An annuity in Swiss francs is not subject to reporting to the U.S. Internal Revenue Service. In addition, the transfer of funds by wire or check are not reportable. Investors can be assured of the privacy of their accounts.

- *Ease of investing.* The Swiss have made management of a Swiss annuity simple. Investors can send deposits to Switzerland in

U.S. dollars via a personal check. Funds may also be transferred by bank wire. It is as easy as managing an annuity purchased and maintained in the United States.

- *Swiss annuities and U.S. pension plans.* Swiss annuities can be included in a variety of tax-sheltered plans in the United States. Some of these plans include IRAs, corporate plans, or Keogh plans. These plans can also be rolled over into a Swiss annuity. Investors have much flexibility.

Protecting Your Assets Through Swiss Annuities

Swiss annuities clearly provide many advantages and benefits to investors over annuities offered in other places. Still, perhaps most important, and often overlooked, is the superior asset-protection aspect of Swiss annuities. This aspect is a crucial point for investors who wish to ensure that their investments and growing wealth are protected from the claims of creditors.

When annuities are structured properly, Swiss law prevents, except in cases where intent to defraud can be proven, that annuities, along with other insurance policies, cannot be seized by creditors. These policies may not even be included in a Swiss bankruptcy proceeding.

Using A Swiss Insurance Broker

The most practical way for North Americans to get information on Swiss annuities is to send a letter to a Swiss insurance broker specializing in foreign business. This is because very few transactions can be concluded directly by foreigners either with a Swiss insurance company or with regular Swiss insurance agents. They can legally handle the business, but they aren't used to it.

JML Swiss Investment Counsellors is an independent group of financial advisors. Since 1974 they have specialized in Swiss franc insurance, gold and selected Swiss bank managed investments for overseas and European clients. To date the group is servicing over 20,000 clients worldwide with investments through JML of more than 3.5 billion Swiss francs. Their services are free of charge to you because they are paid by the renowned companies with which you invest your money. Their commissions and fees are standard, and all transactions are subject to strict regulation by the Swiss authorities.

All of their staff are fluent in English, and understand the special concerns of the international investor. They know about all the many little details that are critical to you as a

non-Swiss investor, and have answers to your tax questions
and other legalities.

JML Jurg M. Lattmann AG
Swiss Investment Counsellors
Germaniastrasse 55, Dept. 212
CH-8033 Zurich, Switzerland
telephone: +41 1 368 8233
fax: +41 1 368 8299; marking your fax: "Attn:
Dept. 212"

When you contact a Swiss insurance broker, be sure
to include, in addition to your name, address, and telephone
number, your date of birth, marital status, citizenship, number
of children and their ages, name of spouse, and a clear
definition of your financial objectives including what dollar
amount you would like to invest.

HOW TO MAKE REALLY BIG MONEY OVERSEAS

One of the most valuable elements of international investing is the ability to compound earnings tax free. This factor alone is a major reason for selecting offshore opportunities over domestic investments.

The Value of Tax-Free Compound Interest

Much of the discussion of the growing value of an annuity investment depends upon the tax free compounding of the earnings.

Everyone knows about the "miracle of compound interest." It is such a cliche that almost everyone ignores the powerful, fundamental truth underlying the concept. And few people understand how to make compound interest work for them.

Compounding is a two-way street. Debts compound, too. That is why so many "wealthy" people are going bankrupt, for example. Back in the 1970s and 1980s, the fashion of the time was to buy real estate leveraged with debt, and roll over the debt, counting on an increase in the value of the property to pay off the debt and make a profit.

And in much of the United States, real estate values did increase at a rate that enabled a lot of people to make a lot of money purely on debt financing. They would buy a property. And they would pay for it with borrowed money, sometimes 90% or more of the total value. (The banks played along with this game. They made money too as long as prices were rising.)

Instead of paying off the loan, they would allow the principal and interest to build. At 10% interest...after a year the principal on a $100,000 loan would grow to $110,000. In five years it would be a monstrous $161,000, and so on.

The trouble is, real estate values don't go in one direction only. They also go down, as is they are now in many parts of the world. All that built-up, compounded debt eventually has to be paid. And very often, real estate investors do not have the means to actually pay off the debt they contracted. They never expected to have to do so.

The secret of compound interest is to be on the right side of it. Debts compound and so do costs. Being on the right side of compounding means positioning investments so that time works for them, rather than against them. When investments are positioned properly, each passing day adds to their value, free from taxes and inflation.

More than 2,000 years ago the philosopher Aristotle explained that the secret of success in anything was <u>habit</u>. Aristotle used the word "ethos." To him it was the crucial ingredient of all genius. And it was nothing more than a recognition of the concept of compound interest applied to life itself.

Aristotle recognized that people do not simply wake up one day with the idea for a great invention...or jump to the command of a great army...or write down a marvelous essay...or get rich.

All progress is made by small increments compounding over time. A great thinker thinks hard for a long time and, over time, comes up with great thoughts.

A great builder lays one brick at a time and, over time, builds great monuments.

A great artist works day after day and, over time, produces great works of art.

So too, a man builds his wealth a little each day...and over time...becomes very rich.

The idea of building wealth over time has a kind of tedious ring to it, but it leaves out the entire power of compounding. With compounding, time adds to value. Instead of being tedious, the passage of time in the investment plan becomes an important ingredient that turns the capital into more.

Thus the "miracle of compound interest." It is based upon a powerful, fundamental truth, although too few people understand how to make compound interest work for them.

The results are incredible. As we showed earlier, a 20% annual free of tax compounds to a sum 1200% larger over a lifetime than the same sum with tax. It is the difference between $8 million and $100 million over 40 years. And the same magic applies when you start with smaller amounts.

But we do want to stress that just because money is offshore does not automatically mean it is tax-free. It is important that a proper and legal structure be used to keep the money tax-free, either through annuities, trusts, or other structures that you choose only after proper accounting and legal advice.

$2,000 a year into a tax-free account investing in stocks that pay 10% dividends, means $35,062.31 after 10 years -- not including any capital gains.

YEAR	TAX-FREE TOTAL	INCLUDING DIVIDENDS
1 starting capital	$2,000.00	$2,200.00
2 add US$2,000	$4,200.00	$4,620.00
3 each year	$6,620.00	$7,282.00
4	$9,282.00	$10,210.20
5	$12,210.20	$13,431.22
6	$15,431.22	$16,974.34
7	$18,974.34	$20,871.77
8	$22,871.77	$25,158.94
9	$27,158.94	$29,874.83
10	$31,874.83	$35,062.31

After 25 years, he'd have $216,363.29 -- just by putting $2,000 a year into his IRA, with its $2,000 contribution limit. An annuity has no such limit.

11	$37,062.31	$40,768.54
12	$42,768.54	$47,045.39
13	$49,045.39	$53,949.92
14	$55,949.92	$61,544.91
15	$63,544.91	$69,899.40
16	$71,899.40	$79,089.34
17	$81,089.34	$89,198.27
18	$91,198.27	$100,318.09
19	$102,318.09	$112,549.89
20	$114,549.89	$126,004.87
21	$128,004.87	$140,805.35
22	$142,805.35	$157,085.88
23	$159,085.88	$174,994.46
24	$176,994.46	$194,693.90
25	$196,693.90	$216,363.29

Compounding this kind of income from investments, in a tax-free annuity, is a guaranteed way to build wealth. There weren't any extra risks, or any extra effort. Once the wealth-building strategy was in place, it was just a matter of time. Most investors are looking for extraordinary capital gains -- and most fail to realize how hard it is to achieve that. Wealth-building investors should seek investments offering decent dividends or interest, and let that yield compound. Think of it another way:

Amounts at Compound Interest

Multiply the Principal by the Factor in the Table

Years	1%	2%	3%	4%	5%	6%	7%
1	1.0100	1.0200	1.0300	1.0400	1.0500	1.0600	1.0700
2	1.0201	1.0404	1.0609	1.0816	1.1025	1.1236	1.1449
3	1.0303	1.0612	1.0927	1.1249	1.1576	1.1910	1.2250
4	1.0406	1.0824	1.1255	1.1699	1.2155	1.2625	1.3108
5	1.0510	1.1041	1.1593	1.2167	1.2763	1.3382	1.4026
6	1.0615	1.1262	1.1941	1.2653	1.3401	1.4185	1.5007
7	1.0721	1.1487	1.2299	1.3159	1.4071	1.5036	1.6058
8	1.0829	1.1717	1.2668	1.3686	1.4775	1.5938	1.7182
9	1.0937	1.1951	1.3048	1.4233	1.5513	1.6895	1.8385
10	1.1046	1.2190	1.3439	1.4802	1.6289	1.7908	1.9672
11	1.1157	1 2434	1.3842	1.5395	1.7103	1.8983	2.1049

12	1.1268	1 2682	1.4258	1.6010	1.7959	2.0122	2.2522
13	1.1381	1.2936	1.4685	1.6651	1.8856	2.1329	2.4098
14	1.1495	1.3195	1.5126	1.7317	1.9799	2.2609	2.5785
15	1.1610	1.3459	1.5580	1.8009	2.0789	2.3966	2.7590
16	1.1726	1.3728	1.6047	1.8730	2.1829	2.5404	2.9522
17	1.1843	1.4002	1.6528	1.9479	2.2920	2.6928	3.1588
19	1.2081	1.4568	1.7535	2.1068	2.5270	3.0256	3.6165
20	1.2202	1.4859	1.8061	2.1911	2.6533	3.2071	3.8697
21	1.2324	1.5157	1.8603	2.2788	2.7860	3.3996	4.1406
22	1.2447	1.5460	1.9161	2.3699	2.9253	3.6035	4.4304
23	1.2572	1.5769	1.9736	2.4647	3.0715	3.8197	4.7405
24	1.2697	1.6084	2.0328	2.5633	3.2251	4.0489	5.0724
25	1.2824	1.6406	2.0938	2.6658	3.3864	4.2919	5.4274
26	1.2953	1.6734	2.1566	2.7725	3.5557	4.5494	5.8074
27	1.3082	1.7069	2.2213	2.8834	3.7335	4.8223	6.2139
28	1.3213	1.7410	2.2213	2.9987	3.9201	5.1117	6.6488
29	1.3345	1.7758	2.3566	3.1187	4.1161	5.4184	7.1143
30	1.3476	1.8114	2.4773	3.7434	4.3219	5.7435	7.6123

Years	8%	9%	10%	11%	12%	13%
1	1.0800	1.0900	1.1000	1.1100	1.1200	1.1300
2	1.1664	1.1881	1.2100	1.2321	1.2544	1.2769
3	1.2597	1.2950	1.3310	1.3676	1.4049	1.4429
4	1.3605	1.4116	1.4641	1.5181	1.5735	1.6305

5	1.4693	1.5386	1.6105	1.6851	1.7623	1.8424
6	1.5869	1.6771	1.7716	1.8704	1.9738	2.0820
7	1.7138	1.8280	1.9487	2.0762	2.2107	2.3526
8	1.8509	1.9926	2.1436	2.3045	2.4760	2.6584
9	1.9990	2.1719	2.3579	2.5580	2.7731	3.0040
10	2.1589	2.3674	2.5937	2.8394	3.1058	3.3946

11	2.3316	2.5804	2.8531	3.1518	3.4785	3.8359
12	2.5182	2.8127	3.1384	3.4985	3.8960	4.3345
13	2.7196	3.0658	3.4523	3.8833	4.3635	4.8980
14	2.9372	3.3417	3.7975	4.3104	4.8871	5.5348
15	3.1722	3.6425	4.1772	4.7846	5.4736	6.2543
16	3.4259	3.9703	4.5950	5.3109	6.1304	7.0673
17	3.7000	4.3276	5.0545	5.8951	6.8660	7.9861
18	3.9960	4.7171	5.5599	6.5436	7.6900	9.0243
19	4.3157	5.1417	6.1159	7.2633	8.6128	10.0197
20	4.6610	5.6044	6.7275	8.0623	9.6463	11.5231
21	5.0338	6.1088	7.4002	8.9492	10.8038	13.0211
22	5.4365	6.6586	8.1403	9.9336	12.1003	14.7138
23	5.8715	7.2579	8.9543	11.0263	13.5523	16.6266
24	6.3412	7.9111	9.8497	12.2392	15.1786	18.7881
25	6.8485	8.6231	10.8347	13.5855	17.0001	21.2305
26	7.3964	9.3992	11.9182	15.0797	19.0401	23.9905
27	7.9881	10.2451	13.1100	16.7386	21.3249	27.1093

28	8.6271	11.1671	14.4210	18.5799	23.8839	30.6335
29	9.3173	12.1722	15.8631	20.6237	26.7499	34.6158
30	10.0627	13.2677	17.4494	22.8923	29.9599	39.1159

How the Dollar Value of Time Helps Disciplined Investors

Below are two individuals who have different attitudes toward investing. The early investor chooses to begin investing $5,000 annually for retirement. The late investor waits ten years before beginning a program.

	Early Investor		Late Investor	
Age	Amount	Value	Amount	Value
35	$5,000	$ 5,524	0	0
36	5,000	11,626	0	0
37	5,000	18,366	0	0
38	5,000	25,813	0	0
39	5,000	34,040	0	0
40	5,000	43,128	0	0
41	5,000	53,168	0	0
42	5,000	64,258	0	0

43	5,000	76,511	0	0
44	5,000	90,046	0	0
45	0	99,475	7,500	8,285
46	0	109,891	7,500	17,438
47	0	121,398	7,500	27,549
48	0	134,111	7,500	38,719
49	0	148,154	7,500	51,059
50	0	163,667	7,500	64,691
51	0	180,806	7,500	79,751
52	0	199,738	7,500	96,387
53	0	220,653	7,500	114,765
54	0	243,759	7,500	135,068
55	0	269,284	7,500	157,496
56	0	297,481	7,500	182,274
57	0	328,631	7,500	209,645
58	0	363,043	7,500	239,883
59	0	401,059	7,500	273,287
60	0	443,055	7,500	310,190
61	0	489,448	7,500	350,956
62	0	540,700	7,500	395,991
63	0	597,318	7,500	445,742
64	0	659,865	7,500	500,702
65	0	728,962	7,500	561,417

The early investor contributed $107,500 less than the late investor, but outperformed the late investor by over $167,000. Let time work to your benefit!

There is also an insurance aspect here that is not shown by the pure numbers. The early investor is protected should he become disabled or a bad economy limit his earning potential. He already has his money doing the work for him.

Using Offshore Havens Legitimately

The words "tax haven" or "offshore haven" bring to mind far off corners of the planet with millionaire populations. This population, of course, spends most of its day drinking daiquiris on the beach, its funds secure in various numbered Swiss bank accounts. Not so. Tax havens need not be the exclusive recluse of the ultra-rich. People of average means need no longer be captive slaves to the politicians in today's modern jet-set era.

As modern governments continue to expand and swallow human rights, deficits and taxes grow. All free-minded individuals must seek a means to protect their assets from this monster out of control. It is legally possible to pay absolutely no taxes. Your government may want you to think otherwise. The media may love to tattle about the misery of a particular celebrity "tax-evader," but a very important point remains unnoticed. While "tax evasion" is illegal, "tax avoidance" is not. This distinction is crucial.

In *The Complete Guide to Tax Havens* (available through most major bookstores), I have covered tax havens from start to finish, without hopping on the bandwagons for the latest "fad" tax havens. (It is not commonly known, but tax havens are just as interested in finding you as you are in finding them.) It explains everything from the basic criteria you should use when assessing a tax haven to how you can put them to work to save you that big chunk of your income whisked off each year by the politicians.

If you want to gain a good understanding of how the government views tax havens, read *Tax Havens and Their Uses by United States Taxpayers* by Richard Gordon. Frequently referred to as "The Gordon Report," this was a 1981 U.S. Treasury Department study prepared at the request of Congress.

Tax havens are one of the most important subjects for an international investor, yet few understand and use them properly. One group discount them as hiding holes for dirty money, which is not a legitimate use for tax havens. Others think they are only for banking money after you have made it. Not true either.

Money grows much faster if a tax haven is part of your planning, and almost any international investor has an opportunity to use tax havens. It is the purely domestic investor, confined to one country, that cannot benefit from the international fiscal loopholes.

Simply stated, a tax haven is any country whose laws, regulations, traditions, and, in some cases, treaty arrangements make it possible for one to reduce his overall tax burden. This general definition, however, covers many types of tax havens, and it is important that you understand their differences.

No-Tax Havens. These are countries that have no income, capital gains, or wealth (capital) taxes, and in which you can incorporate and/or form a trust. The governments of these countries do earn some revenue from corporations; "no-tax" means that what you pay is independent of income derived through a company. These states may impose small fees on documents of incorporation, a small charge on the value of corporate shares, annual registration fees, etc. Primary examples are Bermuda, Bahamas, and the Cayman Islands.

No-Tax-on-Foreign-Income Havens. These countries do impose income taxes, both on individuals and corporations, but only on locally derived income. They exempt from tax any income earned from foreign sources that involve no local business activities apart from simple "housekeeping" matters. For example, in such a haven there is often no tax on income derived from export of local manufactured goods.

The no-tax-on-foreign-income havens break down into two groups. There are those that allow a corporation to do business both internally and externally, taxing only the income coming from internal sources, and those that require a company to decide at the time of incorporation whether it will be one allowed to do local business, with the consequent tax liabilities, or one permitted to do only foreign business and thus be exempt from taxation. Primary examples in these two sub-categories are Panama, Liberia, Jersey, Guernsey, Isle of Man and Gibraltar.

Low-Tax Havens. These are countries that impose some taxes on all corporate income, wherever earned. However, most have double-taxation agreements many the high-tax countries that may reduce the withholding tax imposed on income derived from the high-tax countries by local corporations. Cyprus is a primary example. The British Virgin Islands is another, but no longer has a tax treaty with the U.S.

Special Tax Havens. These are countries that impose all or most of the usual taxes, but either allow special concessions to special types of companies (such as a total exemption from tax on shipping companies, or movie production companies) or allow very special types of corporate organization, such as the very flexible corporate arrangements offered by Liechtenstein. The Netherlands and Austria are particularly good examples of this.

To understand the precise role of tax havens, it is important for you to distinguish two basic sorts of income: (1) return on labor and (2) return on capital.

The first kind of return is what you get from your work: salary, wages, fees for professional services, and the like. The second kind of return relates, basically, to the return from your investments: dividends on shares of stock; interest on bank deposits, loans and bonds; rental income; royalties on patents. It is the second kind of income, income from an investment portfolio, that tax havens are useful for. Forming a corporation or trust in a tax haven can make the second form of income totally tax free, or taxed so low that you will hardly notice. Certain types of businesses can be effectively based in a tax haven. If you publish a newsletter, for example, you might be able to set up the entire operation in a totally tax free country such as the Bahamas or the Cayman Islands. If your income comes from copyright royalties, perhaps on the computer program you invented, the Netherlands is famed as a base for sheltering royalty income.

SURVIVING A TAX AUDIT

The Basics Of Audits

The words "tax audit" have been known to make grown men cry and the brave to quake in their boots. That's exactly the reaction the IRS wants as it uses the 1.5 million taxpayers who are audited to terrorize the 100 million who are not. The facts are that fewer than 1% of returns have been audited annually for several years, down from 1.31% in 1985.

The percentage of returns audited has gone down in recent years, but the total amount of cash collected has been climbing rapidly. Years ago, about 5% of tax returns were audited, but 40% of those audits resulted in no change in the taxes owed. Now only 16% of returns result in no change. That's because the IRS has joined the computer age and has gotten much better at spotting returns that are likely to yield significant tax payments after an audit. In addition, the IRS has found more efficient ways to contact taxpayers. If you fail to report all your interest income, for example, the IRS computer will discover it and send you a computerized letter, untouched by human hands. The IRS reaches millions of taxpayers in this way without an expensive and time consuming face-to-face meeting. A letter or phone call (sometimes a phone call from a computer) from the IRS is quite enough to intimidate most people. Personal meetings are reserved for the worst sinners.

Your chances of being audited depend on your income, your occupation, and the type of writeoffs you claim. Those earning above $100,000 have the best chance of being audited—better than one in ten. The IRS also looks for self-employed professionals or others who run cash-based small businesses. Anyone filing a Schedule C with the tax return is currently on the list of top audit prospects. Small retail businesses are at the top of the audit list right now. So are individuals who claim deductions for personal computers. The deduction for a person computer is very hard to justify, and the IRS is looking hard for these deductions. You are also likely to be audited if you have substantial tax shelter writeoffs or if certain deductions, such as charitable contributions, are too high a percentage of your gross income.

All tax returns are screened by the IRS computer for these and other telltale signs that more tax is owed. When the computer kicks out a return, a human then looks at it to see if the deductions seem legit or there might be a problem. For example, the computer might kick out a return because it has an unusually large amount of medical deductions. But the employee who reviews the return might see that there has been a death in the family, that there is a large family, or there is some other reason to think the deductions are correct. Agents also are trained to look for abusive tax shelter losses that include large net losses and low gross income, large investment tax credits, an election by a partnership not to be taxed as a partnership, the use of a non-operating entity, no answer or a "yes" answer to questions about the use of non-recourse loans, and a partnership with a negative capital account.

The important thing to remember is this: most Americans overpay their taxes because they are afraid of an audit. This is the biggest mistake you can possibly make. All in all, you are likely to be audited someday. Instead of overpaying taxes in a vain attempt to avoid an audit, you should aggressively cut your taxes in every way possible and prepare for the day when you'll be audited. Take all the writeoffs you can that will stand up under an audit.

The initial contact from the IRS will take one of two forms: a letter or a telephone call. If you receive a phone call, under no circumstances should you discuss anything related to your return at that time. The only time you have to talk with an IRS agent is at a designated appointment (if things even go that far) set up at a time and place of your convenience. Politely tell the caller that you don't feel comfortable discussing such matters over the phone but that you'll be happy to respond promptly to a letter.

There are four basic types of IRS audit, and your response should be different in each case.

(1) The first is a simple letter that asks you to prove or clarify a couple of items on your tax return. For example, you might have forgotten to declare some interest income, or your medical expense deductions might be unusually high. This is called a "correspondence audit." A letter audit is quite easy to respond to if you are really entitled to the credit or deduction. All you do is photocopy the receipt or other evidence that proves you are entitled to the writeoff, and mail it to the IRS. Sometimes you might have to send an explanation instead of a receipt. By all means give the IRS what it wants and close the matter as soon as possible. Once you have been subject to an audit of this type, your return for that year is generally closed. It is very unlikely the IRS will reexamine that particular return. But if you delay in responding to the IRS's letter, you could raise the auditor's suspicions and precipitate a more detailed audit.

(2) The second and more serious type of audit is the "official audit." This means you receive a friendly little invitation to meet with an IRS agent at his or her office. This type of audit usually involves several specific issues on your return. These issues will be specified in advance and you will be asked to bring the appropriate records with you. Bring exactly what the agent asks for, no more and no less. Taxpayers who are worried about the issues bring a tax advisor along or send their tax advisor to the meeting alone. Another aggressive, but effective, technique is to postpone the audit until you can pull the records together and consult with your tax advisor.

(3) The third type of audit is a "field audit," and it is very detailed. These audits are conducted by Revenue Agents, the IRS auditors who know the most about taxes. The other audits generally are conducted by the IRS's least experienced auditors, and sometimes are conducted by employees with no tax training. The field audit takes place at your home or place of business. The agent wants to take a look at your lifestyle and your business operation to see if it matches what is represented on your tax return. It is imperative to have your tax advisor at the field audit. Do NOT go it alone! You should also try to get the audit switched from your place to your advisor's office. After all, that is where some of the important records are. Generally on a field audit the entire tax return is examined and compared with other records the IRS has, such as your bank accounts. It can be a very long process, particularly if you are not able to answer the agent's questions quickly. The field audit by itself doesn't mean that you are in trouble or that there will be a serious problem. Field audits generally are conducted for business tax returns and for wealthy individuals with complicated returns. It is easier for the IRS to go to your place and examine all the records at one time, so a field audit is conducted. Also it is useful to examine your lifestyle, the way you act, and the accuracy of your records to determine how detailed the audit should be.

(4) The fourth type of audit is the criminal investigation conducted by an IRS Special Agent. If you find that a Special Agent is contacting you or people who know you, retain an attorney at once.

Whether you seek the advice of an attorney, accountant, or other tax professional before responding to the audit request depends on a number of factors. You have to consider the type of audit involved, your personal knowledge of the tax law and the issues in question, and the complexity of the questions that are likely to be raised. You should also consider whether your time is better spent on more productive activities while a paid advisor talks with the IRS. Some taxpayers also should avoid meeting alone with the IRS simply because they find it difficult not to act either hostile or guilty. After all, that's the kind of behavior the IRS's PR campaign is designed to instill in everybody. If you are one of those people, don't meet the agent alone.

If you decide to attend an audit alone you will find the IRS asking a number of probing questions, many of which seem irrelevant and personal. Some of these are legitimately related to your return: did you supply over half the support of your dependent? Did you use the correct basis for computing capital gains or losses? Can you verify your charitable deductions?

But other questions are designed to pry and intimidate. The agent may ask if you have a foreign bank account, engage in barter, have a safe deposit box, or have ever been audited before. The agent is looking for a lead to some item that isn't shown on the tax return, such as unreported income. You have to be careful when these questions are asked. The auditor probably won't ask them if a third party is present, but will when it is just the agent and the taxpayer one on one. You also have to be careful when the agent asks a question that he could know about only through an informant's tip. This means that the agent already suspected or was told something about you, and probably has already begun an investigation. The agent might have received copies of your bank records and talked to people you deal with. If you suspect the IRS has information about you (for instance, he asks questions about your bank accounts before he's even looked at your records), ask if he is conducting an audit or trying to confirm an informant's allegations. If the agent refuses to answer, you know that he has been told something. At that point you should seek a tax professional's help if you haven't already.

On personal tax returns the agents are told to take a good look at real estate closing costs (they are supposed to be added to the property's basis), dependency exemptions claimed by noncustodial parents, how casualty and theft losses are valued, large miscellaneous expense deductions, gains or losses on sales of income property, sales of residences, expenses for country clubs, yachts, airplanes, and the like. Sloppy or messy returns also get close attention.

Be careful about discussing your audit or tax affairs with anyone other than your tax advisor. In recent years the IRS has established an undercover program. Agents pose as professionals such as doctors, lawyers, and even accountants in order to gather incriminating information from their "colleagues." In one case, an IRS employee actually worked for a California tax preparer for 15 months and discovered $32 million in unreported income. The courts have ruled that IRS employees do not have to identify themselves and can lie if they want. After pressure from Congress the IRS issued guidelines limiting these operations. High IRS officials are supposed to approve all undercover operations, and there must be reason to believe that there is a problem before an agent goes undercover. But the program definitely has not been shut down.

During the audit be open, friendly, and confident. Do not be hostile. Certainly do not be evasive when asked a question. Do not lie, and do not volunteer information that is not asked. A key point: do not tell the IRS what your bank balances were at the start of the year. This allows him to assume everything that went into the accounts during the year was taxable income. You'll have to prove the source of each receipt, such as repayment of a debt or money that was reported last year. If you are asked a question that you prefer not to answer right away or you are not sure of the answer, simply say you'll have to check your records. Then make a note of the question to show you are sincere. Of course, never attempt to bribe the agent, take him out for a drink, or act overly friendly. It only looks like you really do have something to hide.

If the auditor wants to see your bank records, you have the right to refuse. Then he has to subpoena the records if he really wants to see them, and you have 10 days to go to court and state why the records should not be released. Of course, in refusing to release the records you raise suspicion. If you can substantiate where the deposits came from, there rarely is a reason to withhold the records, but you might want to get an advisor's opinion on this.

The IRS is allowed to look at only the last three years' returns, unless fraud is suspected. Usually only one year's return is examined unless you give the agent reason to believe that an item has been mistreated each year or that you have consistently underreported income. That's why you should never object to a disallowed deduction by stating that you've always treated it that way and never had a problem before. Try to avoid bringing up prior returns unless absolutely necessary.

Remember that an audit resembles a bargaining session. The agent is supposed to do everything reasonably possible to get you to agree to any changes he proposes. This gives you some leverage. If a large amount of entertainment deductions are disallowed, you might agree that some of them are not properly documented but argue that the agent's figure is too high by half. He might cut it down to get an agreement. The agent is not supposed to trade issues. For instance, he can't say that improper auto deductions will be allowed if you agree to disallow the entertainment deductions. But you can continue to insist that the auto deductions are legitimate (giving your reasons) even if the entertainment deductions might be high. Eventually the agent might agree to drop one if it seems that you will agree to the other.

When you and the agent agree, you will be asked to sign a Form 870, Waiver of Restrictions on Assessment. When you sign the form, you agree to pay the amount and the IRS can start assessment and collection immediately. You won't be issued a notice of deficiency and won't be allowed to appeal to the Tax Court. If you refuse to sign, you'll be sent a proposed notice of deficiency that gives you an opportunity to appeal within the IRS and eventually to the Tax Court. These steps are explained in the upcoming sections "How to Get Audit Results Reversed" and "How to Take Your Case to Tax Court."

Wondering if the IRS will pick you to audit? UMI Books On Demand has just arranged to reprint a report which has been unavailable for many years. *How The Internal Revenue Service Selects Individual Income Tax Returns For*

Audit shows the basis for IRS audit selection using excerpts from the U.S. General Accounting Office study. To order, send $25 to University Microfilms International, 300 North Zeeb Rd., Ann Arbor MI 48106. Be sure to specify catalog number AU00381 as they have over 100,000 titles in their catalog.

How to Get Audit Results Reversed

Audit agents often make incorrect or unreasonable assessments of back taxes. You can appeal these assessments successfully. You don't have to go to court to beat the IRS. An internal review process known as the Appeals Office has been set up by the IRS to review controversies over audit results. The objective behind the Appeals Office is to settle cases so the IRS can avoid the time and expense of litigation. By taking your case to the Appeals Office, you can win a favorable settlement and also avoid costly court action.

The Appeals Office is not just a rubber stamp of audit agent actions. Appeals officers review the cases fairly impartially and settle unless they believe that the IRS would prevail in court. The goal is for each appeals officer to settle 85% of the cases handled. This goal differs markedly from the auditor's goals of (1) justifying time spent on a case by making a large assessment and (2) closing cases as quickly as possible. Statistics indicate that appeals officers achieve their goals. For instance, the General Accounting Office reviewed the performance of the Appeals Office for 1979 and found that additional penalties and assessments were reduced or eliminated in 60% of the cases heard by the office. In 1982 taxes and penalties were reduced or eliminated in 84% of the cases. In addition, appeals officers are more experienced and knowledgeable than audit agents, so they are less likely to take erroneous positions.

You should not be surprised when audit results are unacceptable, but you also shouldn't be surprised that the results can be changed without undergoing the cost of litigation. Yet it appears that few taxpayers believe this, because very few audits are appealed. Part of the problem might be that taxpayers are unfamiliar with the process.

After an audit, you usually will receive a 30-day letter, known formally as a notice of proposed deficiency. This letter and the accompanying report explain the additional taxes the auditor intends to assess. The proposed assessment will be explained in person when the audit is conducted at your business or in the auditor's office, then the letter will be mailed if you do not agree to the changes.

Upon receiving the letter, you have 30 days to decide the action you want to take. You can agree to the changes, sign the consent form enclosed with the letter, and pay the taxes. Or you can oppose the changes. A third option is to do nothing, in which case the IRS will formally assess the additional taxes after the 30-day period expires.

You appeal a proposed assessment by requesting a conference with the Appeals Office. This can be done with a simple letter to the District Director. (Specific instructions are in the 30-day letter.) In some cases you also have to file a written protest with the request. The protest is a letter that explains your view of the proposed deficiencies. The protest must contain your name and address, the date and symbols from the 30-day letter, the tax years involved, a description of the changes you are protesting, and a statement of the facts and law that support your position. In the protest you also must declare that all facts stated in the protest are true.

A major dispute among tax advisors is whether the protest should fully develop your argument or should be what is known as a skeleton protest that just outlines your position. The fully developed argument is probably best. You don't want to turn down an opportunity to present a detailed defense of your position. You could rely on the presentation made at the appeals conference to make your case, but it is not a good idea to hit the appeals officer with new ideas at what might be your only meeting. The officer might not be able to respond fully because he or she didn't consider the arguments beforehand and might not remember them completely when the conference is over. It is better to fill the protest with all the possible arguments that support you, putting the strongest arguments first.

The written protest is not required when the audit was conducted by correspondence or in the agent's office, or after a field examination when the assessment for a tax year is $2,500 or less. Though a protest is not required in those situations, you should file one for the reasons listed above. It can only improve your chances of winning a favorable settlement. After the Appeals Office receives the protest, you will be contacted to arrange a conference.

The next step is to prepare for the conference. Both you and the appeals officer will enter the conference with the idea of reaching a mutually agreeable settlement. The appeals officer is under instructions to settle the case on terms similar to those that a court would reach. But a case also can be settled under what is known as the hazards of litigation standard. When the law on an issue is unclear or it is uncertain how a court would interpret the facts, the officer can make a mutual concession settlement. This is when each side recognizes the uncertainty of litigation and is willing to compromise so that neither side wins 100%.

To prepare for the conference you must gather all the facts available. Collect all relevant documents and get statements from any witnesses or other participants in the transaction. You will have an advantage when collecting evidence because you have firsthand knowledge of and access to the evidence. The appeals officer, meanwhile, must rely on the file prepared by the audit agent. First determine which facts support your position and which don't, then examine the law on the issue. Avoid using court decisions with which the IRS disagrees. Before going into the conference prepare an outline of each point of law and fact that is in your favor. Also anticipate arguments that the appeals officer will make and prepare responses.

At the conference, you want to emphasize your strongest arguments, especially the facts that are in your favor. Emphasize that your evidence is more substantial and credible than that relied on by the auditor. When the law on an issue is not clear, the IRS wants to go to court with the case that is most favorable to its position. You can prompt a settlement by demonstrating the strength of your facts and convincing the IRS that there are better cases with which to test the issue. Your evidence will appear stronger if you bring copies of all evidence to the conference. Don't force the officer to choose between your word and the auditor's report. Evidence prepared by third parties, such as reports and affidavits, is best.

You should prepare a specific settlement proposal before the conference. At some point during the conference the officer will ask you to make a settlement offer. There must be a separate offer for each issue; appeals officers are not allowed to trade issues. The offers should state the exact amount of additional tax that would be paid. Don't make your best offer first, and emphasize the facts and law that are in your favor when presenting the offer.

If a compromise is reach, you probably will be asked to sign Form 870-AD. This states the agreement that has been reached. You agree not to file a claim for refund for the issues that are settled, and the IRS agrees not to make an additional assessment unless there is a significant error in the agreement. Should you and the appeals officer not reach an agreement, a 90-day letter, or notice of deficiency, will be sent. You can either pay the assessment or take the case to court.

How to Take Your Case to Tax Court

When you're locked in a dispute with the IRS there are several options. You can give in, try for a compromise, or go to court. If you decide to take the case to court, you have three more options: the Tax Court, federal district court or the Claims Court. For most of you, the Tax Court is the way to go. It's simpler, cheaper, and usually faster. So we've prepared this nuts-and-bolts outline on how to take your case to the Tax Court (though we sincerely hope you'll never need to use it).

A taxpayer who is unable to resolve a disagreement with the IRS is issued a 90-day deficiency notice. It is clearly labeled "NOTICE OF DEFICIENCY." You can pay the deficiency, then sue for a refund in either the district court or Claims Court. Or you can file a petition in the Tax Court without paying the IRS any money. You have only 90 days from the date the deficiency notice was mailed to get your petition to the court.

This rule is followed very strictly. Mailing your petition through the U.S. Postal Service is the same as getting it to the court. The day it is mailed will be considered the day the court receives it. But if you use a private overnight delivery service or some other form of delivery, the court must receive the petition within the 90-day period. The case is thrown out if your petition is even one day late, and very few excuses are accepted. One taxpayer mailed his petition on time, but it had insufficient postage and was returned. The second mailing had the right postage but was mailed after the deadline. The Tax Court refused to hear the case.

We cannot overemphasize how strictly the Tax Court enforces its 90-day deadline. Because the court has a tremendous backlog of cases, it does not hesitate to throw out cases on technicalities. We suggest that you make preparations for an appeal to the Tax Court before the IRS issues its 90-day deficiency letter. If you are appealing a deficiency within the IRS and are not confident of reaching a satisfactory settlement, order a copy of the Tax Court rules now. Write to the Clerk, United States Tax Court, 400 Second Street, NW, Washington, DC 20217, and ask for the rules and information on filing a petition to the court. When you receive the 90-day letter, you'll be able to respond right away.

Your petition to the court must follow a form prescribed by the court in its Rules 23 and 34. There's nothing technical or difficult about the form; it's just easier for the judges when all the petitions have similar formats. The petition must begin with basic details about you, the tax returns in dispute, the IRS office that issued the deficiency notice and the taxes in dispute.

Then you need a concise statement of the error the IRS made in determining the deficiency. If you were denied a home office deduction because the IRS says you didn't use the office exclusively for business, you would write: "The Commissioner erred in disallowing petitioner's deductions for home office expenses in the years 19XX and 19XX in the amounts of $X,XXX and $X,XXX, respectively." That's all the court wants -- a very simple statement of what the issues are.

Then comes the meat of the petition, your statement of the facts. Keep your sentences short, simple, and objective. In the example above, you would state what your business or job is, where the principal office is, and details of the activities that took place in the home office.

The important thing is to write in plain English. Don't try to imitate the way you think a lawyer would write the petition. Put the facts down in a logical order, keeping everything simple and objective.

The "prayer" for relief follows. A standard prayer is, "Wherefore, the petitioners pray that the Court may try this case and hold: (1) that the Commissioner erred; (2) that there are not deficiencies in income tax for the years 19XX and 19XX; (3) that the petitioners are entitled to such other relief as this Court may deem just and proper." If you use an attorney at any time during the dispute with the IRS you might also ask for reasonable attorney's fees from the IRS. A copy of the 90-day notice, the tax returns in dispute, and any other relevant documents must be attached to the petition.

The original of the petition must be filed with two copies and a $60 filing fee. You can apply to have the fee waived for financial hardship. A separate statement mailed with the petition can be used to request a particular city for the trial. If you don't request a city, the trial will definitely be held in Washington, DC.

After your petition is filed, the IRS will get a copy and must file its answer within 60 days, though that period can be extended. You'll get a copy of the answer, and it will state which facts the IRS disputes. You then have 45 days to file a reply, but this should be done only if the IRS brought up new issues in its answer.

Often the IRS and a taxpayer will agree on all the facts but differ on how the law applies to them. In such cases, both sides can agree to forgo a trial and let the court make a decision whenever it's ready.

But if a trial will take place, a fair amount of time might be devoted to pre-trial activities. The most time-consuming activity is known as discovery, in which each side tries to learn all the facts available to the other. In most lawsuits, each side engages in discovery. But in Tax Court cases, discovery often is a one-way street, with the IRS asking most of the questions. Discovery can consist of depositions (questioning the parties and witnesses with a stenographer present), interrogatories (written questions to which written responses must be made), and production (releasing copies of documents requested by the other side).

The amount of time devoted to discovery depends on how complicated your case is. If the dispute is mainly over how to apply the law, there will be little discovery; but if the dispute is over the facts or how to interpret the facts, discovery could be rather extensive. In the home office example we've been using, there probably would be a lot of discovery so the IRS could learn exactly which activities did and did not take place in the home office. You could expect to produce logs, calendars, date books, and similar documents in addition to answering many questions about your personal and work habits.

Since the Tax Court tries to make trials as fast and efficient as possible, you and the IRS must "stipulate" facts. That means as the trial date approaches you two must decide which facts you agree on and which ones are in controversy. In the home office example, you'll agree on your name, Social Security number and probably many of the activities that were conducted in the home office during the period in question.

When the case comes to trial, the judge will have read the stipulated facts and can get right into the heart of the dispute without wasting time on preliminaries.

If witnesses are important to your case, you should arrange with the clerk of the court to have them subpoenaed.

The Tax Court trial will be very informal. The only people present will be the judge, his or her clerk, the IRS's attorney (or perhaps two), the witnesses, and you. You can have an attorney or represent yourself. You or your attorney will be invited to make a brief opening statement that summarizes your argument. The IRS will make an opening statement, then you call any witnesses. The IRS will cross-examine each witness as you finish with him or her. The judge can ask questions of you and the witnesses, and frequently will exercise that prerogative. When you are done, the IRS presents any additional witnesses it has. The trial will go quickly because only facts that are not included in the "stipulated facts" will be discussed.

One of the advantages of using the Tax Court is that you don't need an attorney. But there are several times during a case when you probably will want to consult an experienced tax advisor. In particular you might want help in researching and drafting your petition, during the discovery process, and in writing any briefs that are required. This will cost you some money, but you'll still save the very high fees tax lawyers get for court appearances.

One final point that might interest you is the probability of winning in the Tax Court versus the other courts. Each year the commissioner of the IRS issues a scorecard showing the IRS's success rate in the various courts. Taxpayers generally fare the worst in the Tax Court, winning outright only 6.3% of the time in the latest figures. But don't be scared by that figure. Many Tax Court cases are filed by tax protesters or by investors in abusive tax shelters. These people generally know they are going to lose and are just trying to annoy the IRS, so the overall success rate isn't of much use. Instead, take a look at the cases the Tax Court has heard on your issue. The Tax Court frequently gives the law an interpretation that is different from the other courts'. Sometimes it will be pro-taxpayer; sometimes it won't. Obviously, how the Tax Court feels about your particular issue is more important than the overall winning percentages. You or a tax advisor should review the cases on the issue. Then decide if the Tax Court is for you.

Dealing With The New IRS Posture

The IRS is going to be more aggressive and will have more tools to use against taxpayers. Regardless of what else is in tax reform, there are more money and weapons for the IRS. Within a few years there will be widespread changes in the way the IRS works and how it affects you.

The orders for changes in IRS policies come from Congress. There is concern that the computer foul ups in 1985 led more taxpayers to cheat on their taxes in the belief that they wouldn't get caught. Congress thinks more aggressiveness by the IRS is needed to dispel this belief. Congress also has bought the arguments of several former IRS commissioners that there aren't enough audits these days. Reagan's first commissioner, Roscoe Egger, argued that he could afford to audit less than 2% of returns because more sophisticated matching of information returns with tax returns discovers much of the cheating. But Congress has lost faith in the computer system and apparently wants to return to the prior practice of auditing more returns. The tax bill gives the IRS an additional $700 million each year for the next five years. The money is to be used primarily to hire additional auditors. This obviously means more of you will be audited, and some of you will be audited frequently. (Congress also considered this a deficit reduction measure since it is estimated that each dollar spent on auditing brings in an additional seven dollars in taxes and penalties.)

The additional audits might result in more revenue than expected, because Congress is trying to make audits easier for the IRS. It is clear from reading the explanation of the tax reform bill that a deduction will be eliminated and curtailed if the IRS claims to spend an unusual amount of time on it in audits. One of the main reasons given for eliminating the capital gains exclusion is that auditors spend a lot of time trying to determine whether or not particular assets are capital assets. If auditors don't have to spend time on these issues, they can audit more returns.

Many agents also have laptop computers when they go on audits, and those plug right into the main IRS computer. The agent will be able to look at your past tax returns and information returns while in your office. And the IRS is hoping to be able to tap into the computers of other agencies to see what you are telling them.

Congress also gave the IRS more powers. These powers are designed to either discourage you from underpaying your taxes or allow the auditors to really penalize you if there is an underpayment. These powers are so broad that you could be penalized any time you interpret a gray area of the law in your favor, but later turn out to lose the point. The penalties, in effect, could discourage you from taking reasonable positions on your tax return because the cost of not being 100% correct will be high.

For starters, there is an "interest rate differential." Currently, the IRS must pay you the same rate of interest on refunds of overpayments that you must pay on underpayments. But under tax reform, taxpayers pay 1% more than the IRS does. Congress says that banks don't borrow and lend at the same rates, so the government shouldn't either. In addition, the negligence penalty is increased from 5% of the amount owed to 10%. Many tax practitioners have complained recently that the negligence penalty is automatically imposed by auditors, without regard to whether negligence actually occurred. The penalty for fraud is increased from 50% to 75% of the tax underpayment, and the penalty for substantial understatement of taxes is raised from 10% to 20% of the understatement. Congress states that it is concerned that the penalties are not being applied in many cases where penalties are appropriate, and wants to emphasize that these fees should be imposed more frequently.

It is odd that Congress gave these new powers and marching orders to the IRS at a time when complaints of IRS abuse were increasing. In one case several years ago the judge was so outraged at the behavior of IRS employees that he detailed these actions in his written opinion. The opinion was so damaging to the employees that the government tried to prevent publication of it by the private firms that routinely publish all opinions written by federal judges. In a recently concluded case a federal judge found that the equipment leasing firm Omni International was prosecuted through unethical practices and doctored evidence. The case was dismissed. Most tax practitioners can cite similar abuses on a small scale involving their own clients.

Congress held hearings on those issues and decided it had to pass the Taxpayer Bill of Rights. But a watered-down version was passed leaving the IRS with a substantial advantage over taxpayers. So you can expect more audits, more aggressive IRS tactics, and more assessments of additional taxes and penalties. In addition, since the IRS will be hiring so many agents in such a short time, you can expect inexperienced people on the job. This means an increase in mistakes made by auditors, and taxpayers will have to make more use of the IRS Appeals Office to get the mistakes corrected.

So what can you do about this? The first step is to get yourself in the right frame of mind. You have to realize that the IRS is serious about making an example of some people over the next few years in order to rebuild its image as a hardnosed, competent agency. It's an open question whether they will succeed, but you want to prepare yourself in case they do. Here are the actions you can take.

Always have documentation. Congress has tightened the evidence rules for a few items, notably travel and entertainment expenses. And the IRS knows it can always pick up money by asking for documentation from small business owners and individuals with lots of deductions. Discipline yourself to set up a recordkeeping system, even if it is simply throwing receipts in a shoebox or file folder. You don't need a fancy system, but you should have paper to back up your writeoffs. This will be a high priority on audits in the future, particularly where small businesses are involved.

Attach an explanation to your tax return. If you have an unusual item or something that you know is likely to trigger an audit, attach a brief explanation to your return. (First make sure you treat the item properly, or that you have made a reasonable interpretation of the law if the item is in a gray area.) The explanation should show any essential computations that are not included on the return along with a brief written explanation of your justification for the writeoff. Such an explanation might be: "The automobile was put in service on February 15, 1986, and used for business 100% of the time. The taxpayer has mileage records to support the claim of business use." Don't write an essay or tell more than you need to. Usually the auditor will accept your explanation. At other times the IRS will ask you to mail in a copy of the documentation. If it supports your deductions, the auditor is unlikely to spend time looking at other items in the return.

Consider having your return professionally prepared. Most practitioners believe that the signature of a good tax preparer on your return will avoid or reduce the scope of an audit. Auditors generally know the names of the quality tax preparers in their districts (usually CPA firms) and don't waste much time looking closely at those returns. The auditors feel their time is spent more profitably elsewhere.

Recognize that the auditors will be inexperienced. Since no one can learn the tax code quickly, this means that mistakes are likely to be made on audits. Do your best to explain your view of the mistakes and get them corrected early. But be prepared to use the Appeals Office. You also should avoid putting any emotional strain or pressure on the auditor. This is a good idea in all audits -- keep the atmosphere strictly businesslike -- but it is essential with an inexperienced auditor because you don't know what the reaction to pressure will be. Another good tip is to stretch out the audit. An auditor must process cases quickly and might be inclined to close your case if it is taking too much time.

Document your actions and those of IRS employees. One measure is to insist that any statements or agreements with the employees be in writing. Don't accept telephone agreements or assurances. Always ask when you will get a letter confirming the conversation, or write one to the employee. Your letter should summarize the agreement and leave a space next to your signature for the employee to sign his or her name. Request that a signed copy be returned to you or that the employee state any disagreements in writing. One key: Be sure signatures are legible or have printed names beneath them. Some employees are believed to protect themselves by using illegible signatures on all documents. Another good policy is not to meet alone with an IRS employee. Have an attorney, accountant, or even a friend sit in as a witness.

We're not inclined to use scare tactics and we certainly don't want to build up the IRS's image to the point that you are afraid to take legitimate writeoffs. But we believe you should start now to prepare for an audit. The returns you file this year could be the first ones audited by some new employees. Take all the deductions you can, but be sure you can back up these deductions against a more aggressive IRS.

How to Protect Yourself from the Coming IRS Crackdown

Would you like to file your tax return knowing that an audit won't result in higher taxes? It's possible. Tens of thousands of taxpayers do it every year. In fact, in many instances the IRS encourages taxpayers to take this route.

The way to audit-proof your tax return is to get a private letter ruling from the IRS. With a letter ruling you can know what the IRS thinks of your transaction long before an audit agent comes around. You explain the transaction to the IRS, and then it will write you a letter detailing its opinion of the tax effects. You can save a lot of time and money and avoid some headaches.

There are several occasions when you are required to get a letter ruling. An advance ruling is mandatory whenever you seek to change your accounting period, an accounting method, a depreciation method, and in a few other instances. But there are other cases when you are not required to seek a ruling but will find it advantageous to get one.

Anytime you are considering a transaction involving a large sum of money, an advance ruling could be a smart move. Many times the amount of money you will pay or accept depends largely on the tax consequences because the after-tax return is what you are most interested in. If the tax effects could make or break a big deal, you'll want an advance ruling. In a similar vein, you might be able to restructure a transaction in whatever way achieves the greatest tax benefits. An advance ruling will help you do this by explicitly stating how the IRS interprets the law. The more complicated the transaction and the greater the amount of money involved, the more sense an advance ruling makes. In complicated, high stakes transactions such as corporate reorganizations (even of family corporations), the parties often refuse to enter the transaction until a favorable ruling is obtained.

An advance ruling is also a good idea when you know that a transaction falls into a gray area of the law, and you don't want to bother with being audited. You can ask for a letter ruling and report the transaction however the IRS wants. The ruling might even present an angle that you hadn't considered.

But a letter ruling isn't for every taxpayer. If you let a lawyer handle the whole thing, the cost can easily exceed $10,000. The more complicated your transaction, the greater the cost will be. Because of this, a letter ruling isn't worthwhile unless a fairly large amount of money is at stake. You probably don't want to seek a letter ruling when a transaction has been completed or for one that you are determined to complete and cannot restructure -- unless you are willing to report the transaction however the IRS wants.

A ruling request can bring you and the transaction to the IRS's attention and might trigger an audit. (Tax advisors have mixed opinions over whether a ruling increases audit risk, and the IRS won't comment.) For the same reason, you don't want to seek a ruling if research shows that the IRS is likely to give you an unfavorable ruling (unless you can restructure the transaction).

Sometimes you want to avoid a ruling request when you've done something clever. A tax planning scheme that is new will receive special treatment from the IRS. It will be referred to specialists at the National Office of the IRS for careful evaluation and discussion. These specialists will take their time looking for a way to plug the loophole you've found. Some tax advisors believe the IRS uses the ruling process primarily to discover ingenious tax planning schemes that regular audit agents don't have the time or expertise to deal with.

Another disadvantage of a private ruling is the amount of lead time you must allow. The IRS receives tens of thousands of ruling requests per year. Under the best conditions a request will be processed in 60 to 90 days. But if the transaction is complicated or the individuals reviewing the request decide that more information is needed, the process will take much longer. Sometimes it takes a year or two to get a final response from the IRS. Most taxpayers don't want to wait that long.

Sometimes the IRS won't issue a ruling. Each year the IRS issues a rather long list of the issues it will not rule on. The list is composed mostly of issues of factual judgment, such as the value of an item or whether a transaction is profit-motivated. The effects of proposed legislation and new court decisions are also out of bounds.

The IRS also has decided that it will not issue what are known as "comfort rulings." These are rulings that involve well-settled areas of law, but taxpayers want rulings anyway because the consequences of making a small mistake are too great. Instead of issuing rulings in these areas, the IRS is issuing sample forms and checklists that taxpayers can use. The first topic for which comfort rulings will not be issued is charitable trusts. Other areas will be announced as the IRS issues forms and checklists.

A final disadvantage of seeking a private ruling is that the IRS now charges fees for ruling requests. The fee depends on the subject area of the ruling and generally runs into hundreds of dollars. Fees are adjusted each year.

If you decide to ask for a ruling, you must decide how much of the work to do yourself. The ruling request must be fairly long and detailed, so you probably will need a tax advisor to work on at least part of the request. A request that does not contain all of the information required by the IRS or that does not meet the other requirements will be returned, so you want to be sure yours is done right.

The request should be in the form of a letter addressed to the IRS, Associate Chief Counsel (Technical), Attention: CC:IND:S, Room 6545, 1111 Constitution Ave., N.W., Washington, DC 20224. If there is only one issue in the request, send the original and a copy. Send an additional copy for each additional issue. The request must state the names, addresses, and taxpayer ID numbers of all parties involved as well as the IRS district which has jurisdiction over you.

The request also must contain a complete statement of all facts that are in any way relevant to the transaction. In many ways, this is the most important part of the ruling request, because an audit agent can ignore a favorable ruling if the actual transaction differs in some way from the transaction described in the ruling. The description also must include a statement of the reasons for making the transaction. Copies of all documents relevant to the transaction must be part of the ruling request. (Only copies should be sent because contents of the file will not be returned to you.) Although the documents must be included with the request, all facts contained in the documents must be separately stated in the letter. The statement of facts also must contain your analysis of how the facts bear on the tax results.

The next part of the letter should contain a precise statement of the conclusion or conclusions you want the IRS to reach. If there is more than one issue in your request, you can ask for separate rulings or one comprehensive ruling.

The main part of the request will be the discussion of arguments and legal authorities relevant to your case. You also have to identify all authorities that appear to go against your position and explain why they do not apply in your case. The IRS says that if you do not mention the contrary authorities it will take longer to process the request.

Another major part of the ruling request is the deletions statement. By law, all rulings and ruling requests must be available to the public. But confidential and private information are excepted from this requirement. The IRS wants you to identify the items that you believe should not be made public. You do this by submitting a second copy of your ruling request in which the parts you want deleted are enclosed in brackets. This should be sent with your original request. The IRS will review the deletions statement and make the final decisions regarding deletions.

The request also must state whether the transaction described is reported on a tax return and give the status of the return (under audit, on appeal, in litigation). You must also tell the IRS if you asked for a ruling on this or a similar issue in the past. The ruling request should state that you would like a conference with the reviewer -- even if you don't. You want to keep this option open. The ruling request concludes with a "penalty of perjury" statement prescribed by IRS regulations, followed by your signature.

There is a fee to cover the costs of processing the requests, and you should check with the IRS district office for the current amount at the time you file the request.

When the IRS receives your request, an initial review is made to ensure that you've followed all the procedures and included the required information. If anything is wrong, the entire package will be returned to you. When the package is complete, it is sent to the IRS division that specializes in your issue. The employee assigned to your request is supposed to contact you within 21 days after he or she receives the package. They'll usually call you on the phone, give you an informal opinion of how the ruling will come out, the IRS's reasoning, and the likely schedule of the rest of the process. You may also be asked to send additional information. Any opinion the reviewer gives you during this informal contact is not binding on the IRS. You'll also be told whether any changes in the transaction could turn an unfavorable ruling into a favorable one. You might also be invited to Washington for a meeting.

After this the IRS will begin drafting the ruling. You might be called periodically to answer questions or supply additional information. When the initial reviewer is done, the proposed ruling is sent to a superior. At this point, you might be given the opportunity to take part in an informal conference to present your arguments one last time. If a conference is scheduled, be sure to get as much detail as you can regarding the IRS's proposed ruling. The reviewers generally will explain their reasoning over the telephone so you can prepare for the conference.

Anytime before a final ruling is issued you can withdraw the ruling request. You might want to do this if it is apparent that an unfavorable ruling will be issued, because you will have to include any final ruling with your tax return when it is filed. Thus you must report the transaction exactly the way the IRS wants it, or face a sure audit.

Even if you go through this process and get a favorable ruling, you could still run into trouble. As mentioned earlier, the audit agent can ignore a ruling when the actual transaction does not match the one described in the ruling. In addition, the IRS can revoke a ruling when it decides that the ruling is wrong or when the IRS changes its interpretation of the law. But generally a ruling revocation is not retroactive if your transaction matches the ruling, the law has not changed, and you relied on the ruling when you decided to go ahead with the transaction.

A private letter ruling can be a powerful tax planning tool. It can almost eliminate the risk of an unfavorable audit. But the ruling process can be time-consuming and expensive. It's not for everyone, but there are tens of thousands of taxpayers who benefit from private rulings each year.

Suppose You Owe Taxes and Can't Afford to Pay

Owing money to the IRS isn't a very pleasant experience. But it happens to many of us at some time. Fortunately, there are ways to reduce the unpleasantness -- and keep it from turning into a disaster.

The IRS recognizes that a number of taxpayers can't pay their bills on time. So several "easy payment" plans have been developed that allow you to pay overdue taxes in installments. Because of these plans, there's no need to worry about going to jail when you don't have the money to pay this year's taxes. Just file an accurate tax return, enclose whatever payment you can, and wait for the IRS to get in touch.

When a taxpayer's account shows that a balance is due the IRS, a notice demanding full payment within 10 days is mailed. Technically the IRS can seize your bank account or paycheck without a court order if payment is not received within the 10 day period. But the IRS usually gives a taxpayer more time to pay up. Three to four notices generally are sent over a three month period. After the Final Notice is issued, the taxpayer's case will be assigned to a Revenue Officer who will immediately begin levying wages, seizing bank accounts, and putting liens on other assets. (The IRS doesn't need to file a lien to seize your wages and bank accounts; it can get these overnight. But a lien must be filed before other assets can be seized.)

You can owe the IRS money and avoid having your assets seized if you contact the IRS soon after the first demand for payment is mailed. Then you can work out a payment plan. The trick is to know what your payment options are, because the IRS won't always tell you.

When the demand for payment arrives, contact the IRS as directed in the notice and tell it that you don't have the money to pay. You will be assigned to a revenue officer who will want to know if you have tried to borrow to pay your taxes and will ask where you tried. You'll be urged to contact friends and relatives in addition to financial institutions. But you won't be required to prove that a loan request has been rejected. The IRS has to take your word for it.

If you can borrow the money, sell some assets, or expect a cash windfall within 60 days, you should ask for a short term payment agreement of up to 60 days. This extension is available to any taxpayer, and the IRS does not investigate your financial condition before agreeing to it. The extension often can be set up over the telephone. The length of the agreement generally is whatever you request -- up to 60 days. Sometimes a partial payment within the first 30 days might be required if a full 60-day extension is granted.

Interest and penalties will accrue during the extension period, but you will stop receiving payment notices and there is no danger of having assets seized. Interest is compounded daily, and the interest rate is adjusted every six months so it is in line with the prime rate. The penalty imposed usually is 1.0% of the unpaid tax per month.

When you get a short term extension, the IRS will ask for the names and addresses of your employer, your spouse's employer, and your banks. You'll also have to describe and give the location of any vehicles and real estate you own. This information allows the IRS to seize all your assets quickly if you miss the 60-day deadline.

Individual taxpayers who cannot pay within 60 days can get an automatic 12-month installment agreement. This agreement is available only if you contact the IRS within three weeks of the date the final payment notice is mailed and if the taxes owed are below a certain amount. The IRS won't reveal what that amount is. You have to tell the revenue officer you are requesting a 12-month installment agreement. If the amount you owe is too high, the officer will say only that you don't qualify. Then you have to play a game with the officer. You ask, "Would I qualify if I made a $200 downpayment? What about $500?" At some point you'll get the answer you need. You'll get the installment agreement if you can scrape together the downpayment first.

For some reason, the 12-month installment is available only if you know enough to request it. The IRS employees aren't supposed to suggest it. The IRS also won't conduct a financial investigation before agreeing to the plan. Your evaluation of how quickly the taxes can be paid is all that matters, providing your outstanding tax bill isn't too high. If you say you can't pay now but can pay gradually over no more than 12 months, the IRS will accept your offer. You'll also have to tell the IRS where your assets are located so they can be seized immediately if you fall behind in your payments.

When 12 months isn't long enough or your tax bill is too high, your only option is to negotiate installment payments over a longer period. The terms and restrictions on these agreements vary around the country, but there are some general rules.

The IRS will not agree to payments over more than 12 months without being sure that you cannot pay sooner. The other agreements can be arranged over the telephone, but you'll have to go through a collection interview for a longer payment plan. This can be uncomfortable, but it's better than having your assets seized. Call the IRS and make an appointment to discuss an extended payment plan.

Your ability to pay will be determined by an analysis of your assets, liabilities, income, and expenditures. Statements of these items should be compiled and brought to the collection interview. The statements should be as detailed as possible. The IRS wants to know how you dispose of each dollar that comes into your household.

The IRS officer will first determine which of your assets should be liquidated. You'll also be told to sell stocks, bonds, and some unencumbered assets. You might also be told to borrow against insurance policies or existing lines of credit. If you have significant unencumbered assets, the officer might give you a 60-day extension and tell you to borrow against those assets.

If your assets are inadequate to cover the taxes, the officer will analyze your monthly expenditures to determine how much you can afford to pay the IRS each month. He'll decide what your "allowable expenses" are, subtract that from your income, and order you to pay the remainder to the IRS.

Allowable expenses include those for the production of income and those providing for the health and welfare of a taxpayer and his or her family. Health and welfare expenses include housing, food, clothing, medical expenses, and similar necessities. You are restricted, however, to what the IRS considers reasonable amounts. If the IRS decides that your standard of living is too high for your income, you'll be told to cut back in certain areas. For instance, the revenue officer might decide that you go out to dinner too often. If so, he'll reduce your allowable food expenses.

Allowable expenses include payments on secured debts, unless the asset encumbered by the debt is not considered a necessity. Payment on a debt secured by a recreational vehicle, for instance, would not be allowed. The IRS will require you to miss payments on such assets instead of postponing the tax payment further. Unsecured debts such as credit card bills are allowable expenses unless deferring payments will allow you to pay the tax bill in full within 90 days. No payments will be allowed on debts incurred after the collection interview.

If your situation is bad enough, the IRS officer will recommend that no payments be required. This will happen when the officer believes that your financial situation will improve eventually, and that the IRS will be more likely to collect the taxes then.

An extended installment agreement is not automatic and must be approved by an IRS supervisor. So it won't do you much good to ask the officer to bend the rules. He really has little discretion.

No matter what your financial condition, contact the IRS as soon as a demand for payment is received. Individuals who ignore payment demands frequently have their bank accounts seized overnight. If you can't pay the IRS, let them know immediately and try to work out a payment plan.

Your New Rights as a Taxpayer

One of the most significant actions Congress took in 1988 was passing the Taxpayer Bill of Rights. Though this is a watered-down version of what was originally proposed and what is needed, the law makes a number of significant changes.

Taxpayers now have some important protections that were not available before then, and some of the worst IRS abuses now are curbed. More importantly, Congress has sent a message to the IRS. The message is that deficit reduction is not so important that the IRS can do whatever it wants to taxpayers.

Most of the Taxpayer Bill of Rights provisions became effective over the last few months, and the IRS has issued some rules in this area, so this is a good time to review what your new rights are. Here are the major benefits.

Knowing your rights. The first big change is that the IRS actually has to describe your rights in writing at the beginning of an audit or other interview. In the past, many people thought they had to talk to the IRS and didn't know that they could refuse to say anything or turn over evidence. The IRS now gives everyone a copy of Publication 1, "Your Rights as A Taxpayer," to meet the requirement. The publication explains both the audit and collection processes and what your rights are during each process.

Audits and interviews. The new legislation also makes clear that you can be represented at an IRS proceeding by anyone who is qualified to represent taxpayers before the IRS. This means attorneys, CPAs, and enrolled agents. In fact, you are allowed to seek representation at any time, and the IRS is required to suspend an interview if you so request to allow you to consult with your representative.

Most importantly, in most cases you do not have to appear at an audit. That had been the IRS' longstanding policy. But a few years ago the IRS tried to change the policy, particularly when business taxpayers were involved. The IRS manual told agents that taxpayers were likely to make misstatements and other mistakes at an initial interview, so taxpayers should be told to attend the initial meeting themselves even if a representative would be handling most of the audit.

The IRS changed this policy under pressure from tax practitioners, and Congress codified the change. You do not have to appear personally at an audit if you send a representative who is qualified to practice before the IRS and is sufficiently familiar with the facts regarding your return to be able to answer questions. You still can be personally compelled to attend an audit if the IRS issues an administrative summons, but this has to be signed by the District Director or Assistant District Director.

An audit also must be scheduled at a time and place that are reasonably convenient for you. IRS regulations on this will be issued, probably later this year.

You can audiotape an audit, but there are restrictions on this. The recording right applies only to in-person interviews, not to telephone calls. (The law on taping telephone conversations varies from state to state.) You must seek advance approval from the IRS and bring your own recording equipment, and you must obtain permission to record from any non-IRS personnel who will be at the interview. (IRS Notice 89-51).

Ombudsman and Assistance Orders. The IRS Ombudsman is an important change for many taxpayers who have problems with the IRS. A common complaint among taxpayers who have been burned by the IRS is that their problems could have been resolved quickly, but the IRS employees involved did not pay attention to important facts until many months had passed. The result was a lot of headaches for the taxpayers and perhaps a loss of the taxpayer's business.

The Problem Resolution Office was set up a few years ago to deal with such problems, but that office had no real powers. Now each PRO has an ombudsman. This employee can intervene in any IRS enforcement action when the taxpayer is "suffering or about to suffer a significant hardship as a result of the manner in which the Internal Revenue laws are being administered." The Ombudsman can issue a Taxpayer Assistance Order, which is legally binding on the IRS.

If you have a problem that you think requires the Ombudsman's help, you should look up the PRO of your IRS district office in the telephone book under "United States Government, Internal Revenue Service." Call or write the PRO and ask for Form 911. When you receive the form, complete and return it according to the instructions. The Ombudsman will then look into your situation and decide what, if any, action should be taken.

But be warned that the PRO will act only in extreme situations. The IRS recently reported that out of over 50,000 requests for action by the Ombudsman, the Ombudsman had taken action in less than 100 cases.

Liens and seizures. The most important provisions of the Taxpayer Bill of Rights probably are those applying lo liens and seizures. This is where many IRS abuses have occurred and is the area in which taxpayers are most vulnerable.

The IRS now has to give you 30 days notice of its intent to levy your property. The old time period was 10 days. Now you have almost enough time to borrow the money to pay your taxes or present documentation to the collections agent before the levy occurs. The notice of intent to levy also must contain certain specified information so that you know what is happening. In the past, IRS notices have been so obscurely written that people were not aware that they were 10 days away from losing their property. A focus of the TBR is to get IRS notices rewritten so that they are easily understood by a wider range of people.

When a bank receives a notice of a levy from the IRS, there now is a 21-day grace period before the bank actually has to levy your account for the IRS. Previously, a bank was required to execute the levy when it was received. Now you have a grace period in which to convince the IRS that the levy should not occur.

Another major change is that your personal residence cannot be seized unless the seizure is approved by the District Director or Assistant District Director or the collection of tax is in jeopardy. The past IRS policy was that your residence could be seized but would be seized only in extreme situations.

Pensions and other retirement accounts are not covered by the TBR, and the courts are still deciding when these assets can be seized. The IRS policy is not to seize retirement plan assets unless there is no other way to see that the tax is paid.

Perhaps the most important right is that you now can appeal a tax lien notice that you believe was filed in error, and the IRS has to release a lien when certain specified conditions are met.

In recent regulations, the IRS explained how to appeal an erroneous notice of lien, and the conditions under which a lien will be released. Part of the Taxpayer's Bill of Rights said that the IRS had to establish procedures for appealing a notice of lien that was incorrectly filed. According to the regulations, there are only four conditions on which an appeal of lien can be based. One is that the tax liability plus any interest and penalties was paid before the notice of lien was filed. The second condition is that the tax liability was assessed without a properly issued notice of deficiency. The third condition is that the tax liability was assessed in violation of the bankruptcy code. The fourth condition is that the statute of limitations for collecting the tax liability expired before the notice of lien was filed. This appeal procedure cannot be used to contest the tax deficiency the IRS has assessed; it can only be used to challenge the validity of the lien for one of the reasons listed.

You must make an appeal in writing to your IRS District Director, marked for the attention of "Chief, Special Procedures Function." The regulations list the information you must include in your appeal in order for it to be considered. In addition, you must file the appeal within one year after you become aware of the lien. If your appeal is found to be valid, the District Director will issue a certificate of release of lien within 14 days of the finding, when possible. These provisions became effective on July 7,1989. (Regs. Section 301.6326-1T).

Suing the IRS. You can sue the IRS when certain specified conditions are met. The general rule is that a government cannot be sued except when it specifically gives consent to be sued. The government has agreed that it can be sued when the IRS knowingly or negligently fails to release a lien when there was an error in the filing of the lien. The IRS also can be sued when an IRS employee acts recklessly or negligently in disregard of any provision of the tax code or regulations. But you can only recover actual economic damages and court costs under this provision, and your reward is limited to $100,000.

These are the major provisions of the TBR. Taxpayers are no longer faced with a completely one-sided system that is stacked against them, though the IRS still is in a better position than the taxpayer. It is possible that IRS abuses will continue and another TBR will be needed in the future.

PRIVACY TACTICS THAT CAN GIVE YOU AN ADVANTAGE

There are a number of little things that can help you to protect your privacy -- and make your assets just a bit less visible. This chapter highlights several little-known options that you may find useful.

Use A Stand-Alone Telephone Calling Card

Intended for travelers who use calling cards frequently, there is a discount telephone calling card that has a low flat rate for interstate calls, anytime, anywhere in the United States including Puerto Rico, Hawaii, Alaska, and the U.S. Virgin Islands. There are no surcharges, no monthly fees, no minimum monthly billings, and international calling is also available.

The calling card is free, and is a stand-alone card, meaning that a person using the card does not have to change their long distance service. It saves up to 68% over the leading competitors, including prepaid phone cards (most of which are around 40 cents per minute) and was rated by *Money* magazine and other financial journals as a "best-buy."

But it is the "stand-alone" part that makes us mention it here. Because the card can be applied for without having to subscribe to a new long distance service, one can use the card for things like calling overseas banks, and pay the separate calling card bill from a different bank account, or by money order. The record of calls made won't be showing up on your home or office phone bill, so there's no easy to follow trail of calls to an offshore bank or money manager. And since the separate calling card bill can be paid by money order, it doesn't create a credit card charge record which is one of the problems in recharging prepaid phone cards. (And you don't get an embarrassing "out of time" recording and cut-off, which can easily happen on a prepaid card when a $10 card is being used for an expensive overseas call.)

For an online application form, visit http://www.familyhaven.com/shopping/telephone.html

How to Keep The IRS -- and Other Snoops -- Out of Your Safe Deposit Box

A safe deposit box is a veritable necessity for keeping things like offshore bank books, precious metals certificates, bearer securities, cash, coins, etc. Yet a safe deposit box can create its own problems.

One obvious problem is that upon death of the boxholder, the bank is required to deny access to the box until a properly appointed executor and an IRS agent open the box. The IRS will presume that all assets are the property of the deceased, so that if you are holding assets that you have given in trust to your children, they will become part of the taxable estate -- or worse, they may be applied to some debt of the estate. Unreported foreign accounts could even be seized as being part of a crime. IRS agents tend to assume criminality, and you are no longer available to provide an alternative honest explanation.

But there are other safe deposit box problems that are at least as important as dealing with the box upon death. For example, if the box is in one name only, many banks will not honor a power of attorney to let somebody else have access to the box in an emergency, unless the power of attorney is signed in person in the bank. If you are in a foreign hospital, and need to authorize your spouse to open the box, this could become a major problem. Even if the bank will accept a notarized power of attorney, there may be problems in arranging for a foreign notary to visit, then having the notary certificate authenticated by the U.S. Embassy or Consulate, and sending it to the bank.

The solution is to form a corporation to hold your principal safe deposit box. The corporation can change the names of the people authorized to access the box simply by furnishing the bank with an updated resolution form. And a box belonging to a corporation is not frozen by a bank because of the death of a natural person, even if that person is the sole person then having access to the box.

To do this properly, we recommend that the corporation be used only to hold the safe deposit box. This provides the maximum privacy, because the corporation has no activities to cause it to be audited or investigated. Under federal law, even an inactive corporation must file a tax return, but a corporate return showing no income can be filled in each year without having to pay an accountant to do it. (Usually after three years of zero income returns, the IRS sends out a form letter saying there is no need to file further returns unless the corporation begins to have income.)

The other obligation that must be met is to ensure that the corporation is in good standing, so that you don't have a crisis in which the corporation no longer exists because the annual reports were not filed. Delaware is the best state for this, because an inactive corporation only needs to file a simple annual return and pay an annual fee to the state (and an annual fee to its Delaware registered agent.)

Privacy can be maintained by having the registered agent file the annual return with the state, signing it as "incorporator," which keeps the list of officers off the state records. Most large corporation services will not provide annual report filing services, but the one mentioned below will do so. To be entirely safe, one can even leave the registered agent with funds to prepay the state fees each year, thus ensuring that there is no accidental termination of the corporation because of a late payment.

Since the holding of a safe deposit box is not deemed to be conducting business by any state, the Delaware corporation is not required to qualify to do business in the state in which the box is held, thus improving privacy and keeping the existence of the corporation out of the public records in your own state.

Keeping the IRS away is not the only reason to have a corporation hold your safe deposit box. It also keeps a personal creditor from being able to have the box frozen by a court for an inspection of the contents, which can easily happen during a lawsuit or other claim against you.

Privacy and Data Encryption

Your business affairs are your personal matter. Encryption is an electronic procedure that digitally encodes (converts into unintelligible gibberish) and decodes (converts back to readable language).

Today any reasonably powerful desktop computer can encrypt and decrypt messages which the most powerful supercomputers in the world, working together, could not decrypt. Programs to do this are very inexpensive, and already available to anyone.

Most encryption programs take advantage of a mathematically sophisticated encryption technology that requires two different keys, both of which are necessary to decrypt the message. The sender needs only one to send a message. The receiver decodes the message with the second key -- which never needs to leave his computer, where it can be protected by passwords. Although the mathematics are daunting, the program makes the process simple and straightforward.

Examples of everyday uses are a writer who sends chapters of his new book to his publisher; collaborators on an invention working at a distance and needing to keep others from claim-jumping a discovery; paying bills or ordering from mail-order catalogs by sending encrypted credit card numbers over the telephone; an accountant who scrambles backup tapes so that clients needn't worry about lost confidentiality if the tapes are lost or stolen; and attorneys communicating with clients and other attorneys via encrypted documents.

At the same time, the costs of international communications and transportation have declined to the point where even the average individual can afford to internationalize. And countries around the world are competing for that business. You can take advantage of what these countries have to offer to safeguard your freedom and privacy using exactly the same techniques as giant multinational companies.

Encrypted messages can move across international borders without interference, by telephone, by radio, or by courier. A "message" means anything that can be digitized -- a sequence of words, music, a digitized picture, a forbidden magazine or book, etc.

Privacy of electronic communications leads to an ability to do business from anywhere in the world, with anybody in the world.

It is technically feasible to use these techniques to create a totally secret banking system, with account owners identities being unknown even to the bank. Credits could be transferred between accounts from anywhere in the world through encrypted communications. In a world where governments are increasingly subscribing to treaties limiting banking secrecy, and requiring identification of depositors, it is unlikely that this technical possibility will actually occur in the near future. But unlikely is not impossible -- and the time may come when some government permits such a service, or when entrepreneurs sneak it in the back door by calling it a barter exchange instead of a bank. Since everything is electronic, such a service could even be operated from a ship, an orbiting space station, or The Moon. It is only thirty years since the first Moon landing -- who knows what the next thirty years might bring. The data haven may eventually supplement the tax haven.

About the Author

Over the past 25 years, Adam Starchild has been the author of over two dozen books, and hundreds of magazine articles, primarily on business and finance. His articles have appeared in a wide range of publications around the world — including *Business Credit, Euromoney, Finance, The Financial Planner, International Living, Offshore Financial Review, Reason, Tax Planning International, The Bull & Bear, Trust & Estates*, and many more.

Now semi-retired, he was the president of an international consulting group specializing in banking, finance and the development of new businesses, and director of a trust company.

Although this formidable testimony to expertise in his field, plus his current preoccupation with other books-in-progress, would not seem to leave time for a well-rounded existence, Starchild has won two Presidential Sports Awards and written several cookbooks, and is currently involved in a number of personal charitable projects. His website is at http://www.cyberhaven.com/starchild/

End Notes

[1] I.R.C. sec. 2055.

[2] I.R.C. secs. 664(c) and (d).

[3] I.R.C. secs. 170(b)(1)(A) and 170(c); Reg. Sec. 1.644-3(a)(6)(iv); see also Rev. Rul. 80-38, 1980-1C.B. 57.

[4] Rev. Rul. 55-275, 1955-1 CB 295.

[5] I.R.C. sec. 664(c).

[6] I.R.C. sec. 664(d)(2).

[7] Treas. Regs. sec. 1.644-3(a)(1)(i)(b).